Security Basics for
Computer Architects

Synthesis Lectures on Computer Architecture

Editor

Mark D. Hill, *University of Wisconsin, Madison*

Synthesis Lectures on Computer Architecture publishes 50- to 100-page publications on topics pertaining to the science and art of designing, analyzing, selecting and interconnecting hardware components to create computers that meet functional, performance and cost goals. The scope will largely follow the purview of premier computer architecture conferences, such as ISCA, HPCA, MICRO, and ASPLOS.

Security Basics for Computer Architects
Ruby B. Lee
2013

The Datacenter as a Computer: An Introduction to the Design of Warehouse-Scale Machines, 2nd Edition
Luiz André Barroso, Jimmy Clidaras, and Urs Hölzle
2013

Shared-Memory Synchronization
Michael L. Scott
2013

Resilient Architecture Design for Voltage Variation
Vijay Janapa Reddi , Meeta Sharma Gupta
2013

Multithreading Architecture
Mario Nemirovsky, Dean M. Tullsen
2013

Performance Analysis and Tuning for General Purpose Graphics Processing Units (GPGPU)
Hyesoon Kim, Richard Vuduc, Sara Baghsorkhi, Jee Choi, Wen-mei Hwu
2012

iv

Automatic Parallelization: An Overview of Fundamental Compiler Techniques
Samuel P. Midkiff
2012

Phase Change Memory: From Devices to Systems
Moinuddin K. Qureshi, Sudhanva Gurumurthi, Bipin Rajendran
2011

Multi-Core Cache Hierarchies
Rajeev Balasubramonian, Norman P. Jouppi, Naveen Muralimanohar
2011

A Primer on Memory Consistency and Cache Coherence
Daniel J. Sorin, Mark D. Hill, David A. Wood
2011

Dynamic Binary Modification: Tools, Techniques, and Applications
Kim Hazelwood
2011

Quantum Computing for Computer Architects, Second Edition
Tzvetan S. Metodi, Arvin I. Faruque, Frederic T. Chong
2011

High Performance Datacenter Networks: Architectures, Algorithms, and Opportunities
Dennis Abts, John Kim
2011

Processor Microarchitecture: An Implementation Perspective
Antonio González, Fernando Latorre, Grigorios Magklis
2010

Transactional Memory, 2nd edition
Tim Harris , James Larus , Ravi Rajwar
2010

Computer Architecture Performance Evaluation Methods
Lieven Eeckhout
2010

Introduction to Reconfigurable Supercomputing
Marco Lanzagorta, Stephen Bique, Robert Rosenberg
2009

On-Chip Networks
Natalie Enright Jerger, Li-Shiuan Peh
2009

The Memory System: You Can't Avoid It, You Can't Ignore It, You Can't Fake It
Bruce Jacob
2009

Fault Tolerant Computer Architecture
Daniel J. Sorin
2009

The Datacenter as a Computer: An Introduction to the Design of Warehouse-Scale Machines
Luiz André Barroso, Urs Hölzle
2009

Computer Architecture Techniques for Power-Efficiency
Stefanos Kaxiras, Margaret Martonosi
2008

Chip Multiprocessor Architecture: Techniques to Improve Throughput and Latency
Kunle Olukotun, Lance Hammond, James Laudon
2007

Transactional Memory
James R. Larus, Ravi Rajwar
2006

Quantum Computing for Computer Architects
Tzvetan S. Metodi, Frederic T. Chong
2006

Security Basics for Computer Architects
Ruby B. Lee

www.morganclaypool.com

ISBN: 9781627051552 print
ISBN: 9781627051569 ebook

DOI 10.2200/S00512ED1V01Y201305CAC025

A Publication in the Morgan & Claypool Publishers series
SYNTHESIS LECTURES ON COMPUTER ARCHITECTURE
Lecture #25
Series Editor: Mark D. Hill, University of Wisconsin, Madison

Series ISSN   1935-3235 Print   1935-3243 Electronic

Security Basics for
Computer Architects

Ruby B. Lee
Princeton University

SYNTHESIS LECTURES ON COMPUTER ARCHITECTURE #25

MORGAN & CLAYPOOL PUBLISHERS

ABSTRACT

Design for security is an essential aspect of the design of future computers. However, security is not well understood by the computer architecture community. Many important security aspects have evolved over the last several decades in the cryptography, operating systems, and networking communities. This book attempts to introduce the computer architecture student, researcher, or practitioner to the basic concepts of security and threat-based design. Past work in different security communities can inform our thinking and provide a rich set of technologies for building architectural support for security into all future computers and embedded computing devices and appliances. I have tried to keep the book short, which means that many interesting topics and applications could not be included. What the book focuses on are the fundamental security concepts, across different security communities, that should be understood by any computer architect trying to design or evaluate security-aware computer architectures.

The book is also written to be accessible to a more general audience interested in the basic security technologies that can be used to improve cyber security. By understanding the concepts behind the security terminology, the interested reader would understand more clearly the frequent security breaches being reported in the news and be able to critique or even help propose effective security solutions.

KEYWORDS

computer security, trustworthy computing, hardware security, cryptography, security policies, access control, secure protocols, secure processors, confidentiality and integrity

Contents

Preface... **xiii**

1   Threat-Based Design **1**
  1.1   Security Properties.................................... 1
    1.1.1   Cornerstone Security Properties...................... 1
    1.1.2   Access Control 2
    1.1.3   Trustworthy Versus Trusted 4
  1.2   Threats and Attacks 5
  1.3   Countermeasures and Defenses........................... 6
  1.4   Threat Model 7
  1.5   Security Architecture Design Methodology 8

2   Security Policy Models................................... **11**
  2.1   Multi-Level Security Policies............................ 11
    2.1.1   Bell La Padula (BLP) for Confidentiality................. 12
    2.1.2   Biba for Integrity 13
    2.1.3   Examples................................... 14
    2.1.4   MLS Security Levels and Privilege Levels................. 14
  2.2   Multi-Lateral Security Policies 15
    2.2.1   Chinese Wall.................................. 15
    2.2.2   Clark-Wilson 17
    2.2.3   BLP with Codewords............................. 19
    2.2.4   Electronic Medical Records 20

3   Access Control **23**
  3.1   Authentication.................................... 23
    3.1.1   Passwords and Passphrases 23
    3.1.2   Biometrics 24
    3.1.3   Private Keys and Security Tokens...................... 24
    3.1.4   False Negatives and False Positives..................... 24
  3.2   Authorization.................................... 25

4   Cryptography for Confidentiality and Integrity.................. **29**
  4.1   Symmetric Key Ciphers............................... 29

4.1.1 Substitution and Permutation Ciphers 30
4.1.2 One Time Pad 31
4.1.3 Stream Ciphers 32
4.1.4 Block Ciphers 33
4.1.5 Processor Enhancements for Crypto 36
4.1.6 Cipher Modes of Operation 38
4.1.7 Importance of Key Management 39
4.1.8 Computer Architecture Example: SP 40
4.2 Cryptographic Hash Functions 41
4.2.1 Properties of Cryptographic Hash Functions 42
4.2.2 Collision Resistance and the Birthday Paradox 43
4.2.3 Hash Functions for Integrity 43
4.2.4 Keyed-Hash or MAC 44
4.2.5 Hash Trees 44
4.2.6 Use of Block Ciphers as Hash Functions 46
4.2.7 Examples of Use 46
4.2.8 Computer Architecture Examples 47
4.3 More on the Birthday Paradox (optional) 50

5 **Public-Key Cryptography** **53**
5.1 Digital Signature 54
5.2 Non-Repudiation 55
5.3 Public-Private Key-Pairs 55
5.4 Public-Key Ciphers 56
5.4.1 RSA 56
5.4.2 Other Public-Key Cryptography Algorithms 57
5.5 Uses of Public-Key Cryptography 58
5.6 Public-Key Infrastructure (PKI) 58
5.6.1 Public-Key Certificates and Certificate Authorities 58
5.6.2 Types of Public-Key Infrastructures 59
5.6.3 Web of Trust 61
5.7 Efficient Use of Public-Key and Symmetric-Key Crypto 61
5.8 Example: Secure Sockets Layer 62
5.9 Computer Architecture Example: Bastion 63
5.10 Misunderstanding Public-Key Crypto 67

6 **Security Protocols** **71**
6.1 Protocol Notation 71

6.2	Challenge-Response Protocols.	72
6.3	Protocol Attacks.	73
6.4	Real-World Protocols.	74
6.5	Verifying Security Protocols.	76
7	**Summary**	**79**
7.1	Security Applications.	80
7.2	Research Topics in Hardware Security	81
7.3	The Road Ahead	81
	Bibliography	**83**
	Appendix: Further Readings	**89**
A.1	Dynamic Information Flow Tracking (DIFT) Papers	89
A.2	Secure Processor Papers.	90
A.3	Memory Integrity Tree Papers.	92
	Author's Biography	**95**

Preface

There are certain security fundamentals that underlie the design of secure systems for computation, storage and transmission of digital information. It is essential to understand these basic concepts and learn the terminology used by the security community. They will inform our design of secure computer architectures. This book attempts to summarize for computer architects some of the most important security basics, usually taught in separate classes on cryptography, operating systems security and network security.

OUTLINE OF THE BOOK

In Chapter 1, we introduce threat-based design for computer architects, complementing the current performance-based, power-based, area-based and cost-based design approaches. We define the cornerstone security properties of Confidentiality, Integrity and Availability. We also define fundamental access control, as well as other desirable security properties. We define what we mean by a *security-aware computer*, which we also call a *trustworthy computer*. We also propose a systematic security architecture design methodology.

In Chapters 2 through 6, we introduce the computer architect to important security technology regarding security policies, access control mechanisms, cryptographic techniques and security protocols. A unique aspect of this book is that we give examples of how computer architects have used these security techniques in the design of trustworthy computers.

Chapter 2 describes security policy models for both multi-level and multi-lateral security. This helps the computer architect learn the terminology and understand how to think about security policies for protecting confidentiality or integrity. The use of security policy models enables us to focus on the basic concepts, rather than the myriad other details in real-life security policies.

Chapter 3 describes basic access control, comprising authentication and authorization mechainisms. While these mechanisms have typically been implemented by Operating Systems (OS), they may have to be implemented by trusted hypervisors or hardware, especially when the OS is compromised.

Chapters 4 and 5 provide an introduction to cryptography. This is a highly developed field that provides invaluable cryptographic primitives that the computer architect can use. We describe it as a new way of thinking where instead of restricting access (as in many of the security policy models and access control mechanisms in Chapters 2 and 3), the idea is to allow free access to cryptographically protected information, except restricting the access to the cryptographic keys that allow making sense of the encrypted material.

Chapter 4 describes symmetric-key ciphers and cryptographic hash algorithms, which can be used to facilitate protection of confidentiality and integrity, respectively, in computer systems.

Chapter 5 describes public-key cryptography, which can be used to provide longer-term digital identities. Digital signatures, Public Key Infrastructure (PKI), Certificates and Certificate Authorities (CAs) are discussed, as well as the dangers of man-in-the-middle attacks and misunderstanding public-key cryptography.

Chapter 6 presents security protocols, which are used to establish secure communications across the network, and between computers. They can also be used to describe interactions between components within a computer. Security protocols are essential aspects of a security architecture, cutting across its software, hardware and networking components. The use of strong cryptography becomes useless, if the protocols used to interact between the sender and the recipient are not secure.

Chapter 7 summarizes the topics covered, points to some interesting application areas and hardware-related security topics, and the road ahead for designing security-aware architectures.

A reader who just wants to understand the basic security concepts, but not to design a secure computer, can skip the architecture design examples. One who just wants to understand or implement simple cryptographic processing can skip Chapters 2 and 3. However, any computer architect seriously considering designing for security should read the entire book. It describes fundamental security concepts that enable us to converse with the security community and understand how to approach threat-based design.

For expediency, I have often used as examples the architectures we have designed at PALMS (Princeton Architecture Lab for Multimedia and Security, palms.ee.princeton.edu) to illustrate how the security concepts presented in this book can be used in the design of hardware-software security architectures. These examples are very familiar to me and hence easier for me to write about quickly. I also give some examples of other designs and extensive lists of references to related work in some areas. A subsequent book will discuss specific new security research topics for computer architects. The goal of this book is to condense the vast amount of security basics into a short tutorial. Hence, the topics I have chosen are fundamental ones for understanding some of the dimensions and nuances of security, and can inform new work in the design of security-aware systems.

Computer architects used to building systems must now also learn to think about how systems can be broken or exploited by attackers. We need to learn how to design proactively to thwart such malicious acts. The basic security concepts described in these chapters provide us with a rich starting set of ideas and techniques for thinking about the design of new hardware-software security architectures.

I would like to thank my teaching assistants and students in my Princeton undergraduate class, ELE/EGR 386 Cyber Security, and my graduate seminar class, ELE/COS 580 Trustworthy Computing, for their interesting inputs to my lectures and discussions. The book reflects material from some of my lectures in these classes. Many thanks go to Mark Hill who instinctively appreciated the importance of security in computer architecture, invited me several times to write a book on security, and would not take no for an answer. Mike Morgan also provided constant encouragement in getting me to finish this book. Finally, I wish to thank my dear husband, Howard, who makes life fun and supports me so lovingly, whether I am writing a book or not.

CHAPTER 1

Threat-Based Design

Computers have been designed to improve functionality, performance, cost, power utilization, area and usability. With our increased dependence on computers today, coupled with the rise of cyber attackers on our digital information systems, it is imperative that we also design computers to improve security. Design for Security assumes that attackers exist, who will exploit computing systems for malevalent purposes. We call this *threat-based design*. Such design for security should be done concurrently with design for performance, cost, energy efficiency, miniaturation and usability.

What is at risk? National and international security, financial transactions and economic competitiveness, and individual security and privacy are at risk, to name a few examples. In general, assets, that are of value to someone or some entity, are at risk. These assets are defined broadly, and may include Information Technology (IT) infrastructures, critical infrastructures (e.g., the power grid), intellectual property, financial data, service availability, productivity, sensitive information, personal information and reputation.

A *threat* is a class of attacks that violate one or more security properties. An *attack* is an instance of a threat. In order to understand threats and attacks, we first need to define what we mean by security.

1.1 SECURITY PROPERTIES

1.1.1 CORNERSTONE SECURITY PROPERTIES

There are many security properties required or desired in computer and communications systems [1]. Three such properties have been called *cornerstone* security properties:

- Confidentiality

- Integrity

- Availability

The acronym, CIA, is easy to remember since it is also the acronymn for a well-known U.S. agency.

Confidentiality is the prevention of the disclosure of secret or sensitive information to unauthorized users or entities. *Integrity* is the prevention of unauthorized modification of protected information without detection. *Availability* is the provision of services and systems to legitimate users when requested or needed. Availability is also a goal in providing reliable, dependable or fault-tolerant systems except that availability, in the security sense, has to also consider intelligent attackers with malevolent intent, rather than just device failures and faults. The characteristics of the latter are more easily modeled, whereas attackers' behavior is typically very hard to model with probability distributions.

It is hard to say which of confidentiality, integrity or availability is the most important. Confidentiality is the most important for secret, sensitive, private or proprietary information. Breaches of confidentiality, today, can be more serious than before, because once secret information is posted publicly on the Internet, it can be available to anyone in an instant, and it can never be erased.

While the confidentiality of one's bank account balance may be important, its integrity is even more important—you would not want your account balance to be changed by some malicious party.

Availability may be the most important security property for critical tasks, e.g., those that impact national security or economic competitiveness. For example, when stock-brokers need to make online stock trades, availability of the Internet and online trading services (or its converse, *denial of service*, *DOS*) can result in very significant differences in profit or loss.

1.1.2   ACCESS CONTROL

Protecting the confidentiality, integrity or availability of sensitive information is often related to restricting access to it to only those allowed to access that information, also called *access control*. For example, you use a secret password to *authenticate* yourself to a computer system in order to gain access to its resources and the documents stored on it. A system administrator logging on to the same system will be *authorized* to perform more functions than the average user. Hence, we say that *access control* ensures that only *authenticated* users who are *authorized* to access certain information can in fact access that material, while denying access to unauthorized parties.[1]

Authentication answers the question "Who goes there?" Let's say the person is authenticated to be John Bates. Authorization answers the question "What is John Bates allowed to do?". Together, authentication and authorization are two essential components of controlling legitimate access to a protected object, which can be information, data, code or other resources of a computer system. The acronym AAA (triple A, also an acronym for Automobile Association of America) can help us remember these essential security mechanisms: Access control, comprising Authentication and Authorization (AAA). Authentication and authorization can apply to computers, devices and programs, and does not refer only to humans.

Table 1.1 lists the cornerstone security properties as well as several other desirable security properties. It is important to know the scope of security properties that are desirable, even though

---

[1]   We prefer the definition of access control comprising the components of authentication and authorization, whereas some security experts use access control and authorization synonymously.

in the rest of this tutorial, we focus on only the cornerstone security properties of Confidentiality, Integrity and Availability.

Table 1.1: Security properties

Security Property	Description
Confidentiality	Prevent the disclosure of secret or sensitive information to unauthorized users or entities
Integrity	Prevent unauthorized modification of protected information without detection
Availability	Provision of services and systems to legitimate users when requested or needed
Access control	Restrict access to only those allowed to access the information; comprises Authentication and Authorization
Authentication	Determine who a user or machine is
Authorization	Determine what a given subject is allowed to do to a given object
Attribution	The ability to find the real attackers when a security breach has occurred
Accountability	Holding parties (e.g., vendors, operators, owners, users and systems) responsible for (software, hardware, protocol, network or policy) vulnerabilities that enable successful attacks
Audit	Keeping logs to enable re-tracing events and accesses to protected data or services
Attestation	The ability of a system to provide some non-forgeable evidence to a remote user (e.g., of the software stack it is currently running)
Non-repudiation	The ability to ensure that a user cannot deny that he has made a certain request or performed a certain action
Anonymity	The ability to perform certain actions without being identified, tracked or authenticated
Privacy	The right to determine how one's personal information is to be distributed

We have defined security properties and attributes very broadly to include also properties like privacy and anonymity, which are often listed separately from security. Note that some security properties are at odds with each other. For example, anonymity and authentication may be at odds. Note that anonymity is also very good for attackers.

While the terms "confidentiality" and "privacy" are sometimes used interchangeably in the literature, we strongly recommend that they be distinguished as follows: confidentiality is the *obligation* to protect secret or sensitive information, while privacy is the *right* to determine how one's personal information is distributed or re-distributed.

1.1.3   TRUSTWORTHY VERSUS TRUSTED

Ideally, a *secure computer system* provides at least the three cornerstone security properties of Confidentiality, Integrity and Availability. However, this is often not possible nor necessary, and providing different subsets (or supersets) of these may be sufficient in many scenarios. We discuss this further later in this chapter and throughout the book.

A *trustworthy computer* is one that is *designed* to be dependable and to provide security properties, to do what it is supposed to do and nothing else that may harm itself or others. In contrast, what has been proposed in the past is a *trusted computer*, i.e., one that is depended upon to enforce a security policy. If a trusted computer (or trusted person) is compromised, then all bets are off for enforcing the security policy. A trusted computer may not be trustworthy, and vice versa.

For example, a general is trusted, but a corrupted general who leaks secrets to enemies, is not trustworthy. Because of this, the security policies that depend on the general being trusted may be breached. Similarly, a computer system is sometimes (blindly) said to be trusted to keep certain information confidential, but it may never have been designed to be trustworthy in the first place. Unfortunately, this is the case with commodity computers ubiquitously used today.

For computer systems, the term *trusted computing base* (TCB) refers to the set of hardware and software components that if violated, implies that the security policies may not be enforced. Unfortunately, no COTS (Commodity Off The Shelf) computer system today can achieve a dependable trusted computing base. In fact, COTS computers just have not been designed to be trustworthy. Security has typically been bolted on, after the fact, resulting in degradation of performance, cost, time-to-market and ease-of-use.

For future COTS computers to be trustworthy, we need computer architects who understand security issues. Today, security issues are not taught in the core hardware or software curriculum in U.S. colleges. It is essential that we remedy this, and educate computer architects, systems designers and students to understand, research, design and develop trustworthy computer systems.

Since it is very difficult, or almost impossible, to guarantee that large and complex software and hardware systems are completely free of bugs and security vulnerabilities, it is desirable to make the Trusted Computing Base (TCB) as small as possible, to maximize the chance that it is correct and free of security vulnerabilities. The *attack surface* of an entity (e.g., the TCB) refers conceptually to the area through which an attacker can penetrate the entity; the means and path of a particular peneration is called an *attack vector*. A smaller TCB reduces the attack surface of the TCB and the attack vectors which an adversary could use to penetrate the system, compromise its integrity or steal its secrets. Furthermore, smaller trusted software components are much more amenable to formal verification techniques than large, complex software components.

1.2   THREATS AND ATTACKS

A *security breach* is an event that violates a security property. For example, it could be a breach of confidentiality, of integrity or of availability, etc. A security breach can be intentionally caused or accidental.

A *threat* is any action that can damage an asset, or cause a security breach. For example, there are disclosure threats, modification threats and denial of service threats, which threaten the main security goals of protecting confidentiality, integrity and availability, respectively.

An *attack* is a specific instance of a threat. It involves detailed descriptions of the system, the vulnerabilities exploited, the attack path and the assets attacked.

A *vulnerability* is a weakness in a system that can be exploited to cause damage to an asset. One or more vulnerabilities are exploited in an attack.

A list of threats and example attacks are given in Table 1.2. Some of these attacks are obvious from their names, while others are described in detail in later chapters. The list and examples are meant to be illustrative rather than comprehensive. Most of the attacks, in the end, lead to a breach in confidentiality, integrity or availability. While we do not describe each of these attacks here, interested users can easily find their descriptions via a Google search. The goal here is just to illustrate the broad range of attacks that have been seen.

Table 1.2:   Examples of Threats and Attacks

Threats	Examples of Attacks
Confidentiality breaches	Eavesdropping; key-logging; password cracking; secondary dissemination by authorized recipients; leaking information through covert channels or side channels
Integrity breaches	Undetected modifications of data or programs; spoofing attacks; splicing attacks; replay attacks; corrupting audit logs, or other mechanisms for attribution, accountability and security
Availability breaches	Packet dropping; Denial of Sevice (DoS) attack; distributed Denial of Service attack (DDoS); network flooding; resource depletion
Authentication threats	Masquerading, impersonation; identity theft

Privacy breaches	Leaking sensitive personal information, e.g., medical record, salary, browsing habits, etc.
Anonymity breaches	Tracing tools that can accurately identify an individual, entity or machine
Insider threats	Attacker is an authorized person who knows the system well, e.g., a software or hardware designer, system administrator; covert channel attacks
Hardware attacks	Physical attacks; attacks on hardware; side-channel attacks; hardware Trojans
Software attacks	Attacks on software; operating system attacks; hyperviser attacks; API attacks; web attacks, e.g., cross-site scripting attacks; malware, e.g., viruses, worms and Trojans
Protocol attacks	Man-in-the-middle attacks; reflection attacks; replay attacks; IP spoofing attacks
Network-enabled threats	Virus attacks; worm attacks; DDoS attacks; firewall attacks; intrusions; protocol attacks
Other types of attacks	Byzantine attacks; script kiddie attacks

In order to defend successfully against attacks, we need to understand the attacker's motivations and how he thinks. "Know thy enemy" is an important defense strategy and an important part of threat-based design.

The term "black-hat hacker" is used for someone who performs attacks for malicious purposes, while "white-hat hacker" is used for someone who thinks like an attacker, proposes or even carries out some part of an attack in order to alert organizations to shore up their defenses.

Cyber attackers have evolved from hackers performing attacks for fun and fame, to criminal entities that use cyber attacks for extortion or fraud, to high-end cyber attackers with deep pockets and sophisticated skills. These may be cyber terrosist groups that may try to bring down critical infrastructures like the electricity grid, or nation-state attackers with the capability to launch cyber warfare. Hence, the stakes are much higher and the attackers are more powerful. Furthemore, attacks have been automated, so that one does not have to be an expert programmer nor very knowledgeable about the system to launch a successful attack. Some of these authomated attacks are sometimes called *script kiddie attacks*.

1.3   COUNTERMEASURES AND DEFENSES

A *countermeasure* is a defense against an attack. The term indicates the reactive stance of security measures in the past: after an attack occurs, we propose a countermeasure (and hopefully implement this). A more proative stance is necessary moving forward. The terms "threats and defenses" and "attacks and countermeasures" are frequently used together.

Defenses against attacks can be characterized as detection, prevention, mitigation, recovery and forensic defenses. One can try to detect vulnerabilities in systems and try to remove these. One can try to prevent attacks from happening. After an attack has started, one can try to mitigate the impact of the attack. After a successful attack, one can try to recover from the attack as quickly and completely as possible, and in general, respond to the attack. Finally, it is useful to design mechanisms to collect forensic evidence and enable proper attribution of the attack.

It may be useful to remark that confidentiality attacks are hard to recover from: when the cat is out of the bag, or the horse has left the barn, it is too late.

1.4   THREAT MODEL

Different usage scenarios require different types and levels of security. There are also many different types of assets that need to be protected against different levels of threats. For example, protecting against illegitimate downloading of a movie rental has significantly different security requirements than protecting against the loss of nuclear weapons' secrets. The greater the risk of damages and the more valuable the assets to be protected, the greater the degree of security protection needed. Since it is not possible, nor desirable, to design a one-size-fits-all secure computer, it is essential to specify clearly the threat model in the design of a computer system and in its evaluation.

A *threat model* specifies the types of threats that the system defends against, and which threats are not considered. For example, in certain usage scenarios, preventing confidentiality breaches is essential while availability is not specifically considered. This means that even if a Denial of Service attack occurs, the sensitive information must not be disclosed to an attacker. For example, the confidential information may be encrypted with the encryption key unavailable to the attacker, or the information may be automatically erased upon an attack. This is also called a *fail-safe* strategy for confidentiality protection.

A threat model would also specify whether attacks on the operational system in the field are the only ones considered, or whether the system also considers attacks during the development of the system, e.g., by a systems programmer or hardware designer. These are called *operational attacks* versus *developmental attacks*, respectively. Developmental attacks are a class of *insider attacks*, which are typically much harder to protect against, since the designer (an insider) is actually building in a back-door or information leak mechanism in the system. Implementations of the system will be verified according to the design[2] and thus verified correct, since the back-door vulnerability is part of the design.

---

[2]   For example, a hardware chip design becomes the golden netlist for verifying different levels of fabrication of the chip.

Threats can also be said to be *active* or *passive*. For example, eavesdropping on the public Internet or wireless networks is a passive attack, whereas modifying the information being sent on such networks is an active attack.

The threat model could be concerned only with attacks on the software, or also on the hardware. The powerful system software, like the Operating System and the Hyperviser, which control system resources, could also be compromised (i.e., attacked and corrupted) by attackers. Thus the threat model could include attacks from a malicious or compromised Operating System or Hypervisor.

Some attacks are known, and *attack signatures*, which characterize the attack, or variants of the attack, have been developed and can be used to identify the attack. For example, virus scanners are examples of defenses that use a database of virus signatures to detect virus infections in a computer system. Other attacks have never been seen before, and are called *zero-day attacks*. A threat model could specify if zero-day attacks are targeted or not considered.

A threat model should clearly specify what assumptions are being made about the system, its users and the power of the attackers. It should specify which types of threats are considered and which are not. A threat model need not describe the details of the attacks that it protects against.

1.5   SECURITY ARCHITECTURE DESIGN METHODOLOGY

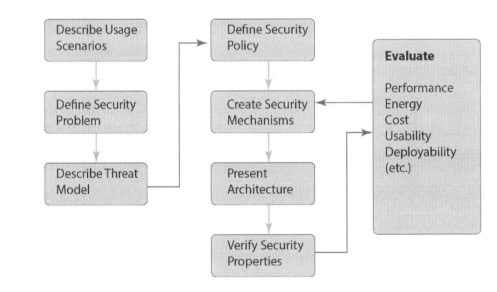

Figure 1.1: Security architecture design methodology.

Figure 1.1 shows our recommended methodology for designing secure computer systems, especially those with new hardware security mechanisms or features. It shows how we can incorporate threat-based design into the computer design process.

First, describe the usage scenarios that you are designing for. Then, the security problem should be defined clearly and succinctly—ideally in one sentence. Next, the threat model should be defined to clarify which threats the solution will address, and also those threats that are not considered and why. Often, in a particular usage model, certain threats are very unlikely or much lower in priority than other threats. Then a security policy (or a range of policies) should be defined that fits the usage scenarios and defends against the threats in the threat model when the appropriate policy is correctly enforced. (We discuss security policies in a later chapter.)

The solution may involve enhancing existing architectures or creating new architectues to enforce the required security policies, thus defending against the threats considered in the threat model. These are called *security mechanisms* by the security community. They are what we would call security architecture features, in the architecture community.

Security policies lay down the rules for protecting the desired security properties, providing the desired security properties and defending against attacks, while security mechanisms are designed to enforce these security policies. If the wrong security policy is defined, then no amount of security mechanisms can prevent security breaches. Similarly, even if the most comprehensive and correct security policy is defined, this is of no use if there are no security mechanisms that can enforce it. Security mechanisms are implemented in any layer of software, hardware or networking, in a computer or across a distributed computer system.

These security mechanisms should ideally be part of the initial design of the computer. Often, they can also be integrated into existing designs. The entire architecture is then presented. It is important to ensure that performance, power, area, cost and usability goals are also satisfied, in addition to the security goals. Otherwise, users will choose higher performing or more energy-efficient (battery preserving) or lower cost computers over more secure ones. Hence, in designing trustworthy computers, a goal I suggest (which my students sometimes call "Lee's mantra") for *security-aware architectures*:

> *"Security without compromising performance,*
> *power consumption, cost and usability."*

While this is often not attainable except for specific problems, we challenge the creative computer architecture community to come up with very clever solutions that meet this goal.

The security properties provided by the new architecture should be carefully verified at design time. This is a new aspect of design verification for which new tools and methodologies need to be developed. The formal verification techniques that have been developed for security verification are currently not scalable to complex software-hardware systems. In fact, most tools work for software-only designs, or hardware-only designs, but not for a software-hardware architecture.

The design must also be evaluated for performance, power, area, cost, usability and deployability. If the new security mechanisms severely degrade the market requirements of high performance, low power, etc., the design should be iterated—as shown in Figure 2.1. Many secure systems have not been successful because they sacrificed market drivers like performance, long battery life and ease-of-use.

How a new secure computer architecture impacts the use of existing software programs and software-hardware ecosystems will also affect the ease with which it can be deployed and used.

We define *security verification* as done at design time, whereas security evaluation is typically done on a finished product or system. Good security practices dictate that security verification or evaluation should not be done by the design team. In order to allow creative human attackers to stress a system, a strategy denoted "red team, black team" testing is often used. This pits a team of attackers against a team of defenders of the system.

CHAPTER 2

Security Policy Models

Security policies in the real world can be very complex. They are often developed by committees representing the interests of the various stake-holders, and/or by executives of a company. Security policies are not technical issues decided by engineers. Rather, engineers design the security mechanisms that enforce the security policies.

Security policy models enable us to reason about security policies. They are abstractions which allow us to see the main ideas in the protection model, while abstracting away the complications encountered in a specific security policy.

In this chapter, we will discuss multi-level security (MLS) policy models (Section 2.1), as well as multi-lateral security policy models (Section 2.2). These are graphically depicted in Figure 2.1. Good discussion of security policies can be found in [6, 7, 8, 9].

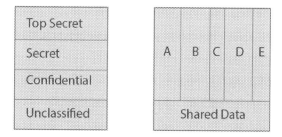

Figure 2.1: Multi-level security (left) vs. multi-lateral security policies (right).

2.1 MULTI-LEVEL SECURITY POLICIES

Multi-Level Security (MLS) policies assume a hierarchical access model, where subjects and objects are classified into different levels of security or integrity. Strict rules describe the allowed direction of information flow, based on these a priori classifications.

As shown in Figure 2.1 on the left, the Department of Defense has four levels of classification of objects: Top Secret (TS), Secret (S), Confidential (C) and Unclassified (U). Similarly, subjects are said to have clearances at four levels: TS, S, C and U. The public is at the Unclassified level, and clearances for each higher level of security require more extensive background checks. These four security levels form a partial order:

$$TS \geq S \geq C \geq U \qquad (1)$$

Someone with a TS clearance can access all objects, whereas someone with an S clearance can only access objects classified at S or lower. While initially designed for the military, MLS policies can also apply to companies, where for example, the executives (TS) can access more company proprietary information than the managers (S), who can access more than employees (C), who can access more than the public (U).

There are separate rules for confidentiality and for integrity. We discuss these below as the Bell La Padula (BLP) security policy model for protecting confidentiality and the Biba model for protecting integrity.

2.1.1   BELL LA PADULA (BLP) FOR CONFIDENTIALITY

BLP is an MLS policy model for protecting confidentiality [2]. Confidentiality deals first and foremost with accessing objects by reading them. Then, writing must also be managed, since this can leak information to others who are otherwise not authorized to read the information. BLP (named after the inventors) has two rules, as shown in Table 2.1. L(x) is the confidentiality level of the clearance or classification of x.

The read rule, also called the "Simple Security property" is easy to understand. One may not read documents that are classified at a higher security (confidentiality) level than one's clearance allows.

Table 2.1: BLP security policy model

BLP Read rule: A subject A with clearance level L(A) may only have read access to objects classified at that level or lower: Subject A may read object B if $L(A) \geq L(B)$
BLP Write rule: A subject A may only write to objects classified at his clearance level or higher: Subject A may write object B if $L(A) \leq L(B)$
BLP Summary: "No read up, no write down"

The write rule, also called the **-property* (pronounced "star" property), is harder to understand. I will explain this with an example. Consider a corrupted general with clearance of Top Secret (TS), who is communicating with someone suspected to be a Russian spy, who would have a clearance of Unclassified (U). Since the general can read Top Secret documents, if he is allowed to write down to an Unclassified document, the spy can then read the Unclassified document which may contain some of the Top Secret information the general has read. The *-property prevents such information leaks. (This is also an example of a subject, viz. the general, who is trusted, but not trustworthy.)

BLP has a "high water mark" effect when two or more objects of different security levels are combined: the combined object has the highest security classification of any of the objects.

As a recent example, consider the Wiki Leaks case. Had a strict BLP security policy been enforced, Top Secret files would not have been accessible by the soldier (unless he had TS clearance). If he had TS clearance, the *-rule would prevent him from writing the information to an Unclassified document, storage or network channel, and he would not then be able to leak the TS information to Wiki Leaks. Of course, the real story is more complicated.

2.1.2   BIBA FOR INTEGRITY

Biba is a Multi-Level Security (MLS) policy model for protecting integrity [3]. Integrity clearances of subjects and integrity classifications of objects can be different from their confidentiality clearances and classifications. For example, a highly confidential document classified at TS for confidentiality may come from sources that may not have been fully vetted, and hence the document may only have an integrity classification of C or U.

Table 2.2 summarizes the Biba security policy model. The "no write up" rule is so that documents of high integrity are not modified or created by subjects of low integrity. The "no read down" rule is to prevent a high integrity subject's information for decision-making from being contaminated by low-integrity information.

When combining two objects of different integrity levels, a "low water mark" principle results: the combined object has the lowest integrity of any of the objects from which it is composed.

Often, just two levels of integrity are sufficient: Hi and Lo. The same can be true for confidentiality levels. In general, an MLS system can define any number of confidentiality or integrity levels, with two as the minimum number: trusted or not trusted.

Table 2.2: Biba security policy model

Biba Write rule: A subject A with integrity-clearance level I(A) may only have write access to objects classified at that integrity level or lower: Subject A may write object B if $I(A) \geq I(B)$
Biba Read rule: A subject A may only read objects classified at his integrity level or higher: Subject A may read object B if $I(A) \leq I(B)$
Biba Summary: "No write up, no read down"

Comparing BLP and Biba

BLP protects confidentiality, while Biba protects integrity. BLP is more concerned with Reads, while Biba is more concerned with Writes. BLP and Biba are duals, as can be seen in Table 2.3.

Table 2.3: Comparing BLP and Biba MLS policies

BLP	Biba
Protect Confidentiality	Protect Integrity
main concern: Reads	main concern: Writes
No Read Up, No Write Down	No Write Up, No Read Down
High Water Mark	Low Water Mark

2.1.3   EXAMPLES

As an example, BLP can be used to prevent malware from reading the password file. Classify the password file as Hi security and anything coming in from the network (or being written to the network) as Lo security. Even if malware (Lo security) gets into the system, if BLP is enforced, it would not be able to read the password file. If the malware somehow manages to assume the clearance of a Hi system program, it would be able to read the password file. However, it would not be able to write the password file to the network, since this would be equivalent to writing to a Lo document.

Similarly, Biba can be used to prevent unauthorized modification of a system file. Suppose system files are classified as Hi integrity and network input and output as Lo integrity. Malware from the network (Lo integrity) would not be able to write (modify) system files, due to the "no write up" rule. If malware is combined with a system file, it will pull the system file down to Lo integrity—hence, the system file will be "tainted" and would no longer be able to access the system data as it could before it was contaminated.

Many papers on Dynamic Information Flow Tracking (DIFT) have been written about tainting data or code from the network as untrustworthy, and propagating this taint—without saying that this is just an implementation of the Biba security policy model. We give a hardware-centric list of DIFT papers in Appendix: Further Readings, as well as a few classic static information flow tracking papers, for the interested reader.

2.1.4   MLS SECURITY LEVELS AND PRIVILEGE LEVELS

It is important to understand that these MLS security levels are not the same as Privilege Levels (PL) in computer architecture terminology. While both define hierarchical access rights, privilege levels do not distinguish between reads and writes. Also, a privileged level (e.g., OS at PL=0) has read and write access to all objects at its own or less privileged levels (e.g., user space at PL=3, or middleware at PL=1 or 2). The MLS security levels are orthogonal to privilege levels. Should an OS have rights to read Top Secret documents? Ideally not, especially if it is not in the Trusted Computing Base (TCB). If the OS is in the TCB, it could be given access to all documents. Since access control is normally enforced by the OS (if at all) for commodity systems, we can say that these OS are trusted but not necessarily trustworthy. Hence, there is a need for a lower level trusted software below the OS, so that the OS need not be trusted. However, this lower level system software, e.g., a hypervisor, can also be compromised—hence, hardware architecture may need to help. Of course, hardware can also be compromised, but attacking hardware is, in general, orders of magnitude harder than attacking software.

2.2 MULTI-LATERAL SECURITY POLICIES

While many military and commercial entities have hierarchical organizations for which MLS policies can apply, many other entities have a need for lateral, rather than hierarchical, isolation of data from different trust domains (see Figure 2.1). This is especially true for many commercial companies. Even in most systems using hirerachical MLS policies, multi-lateral divisions within a security level are often needed. These are due to "need to know" situations, which we describe in Section 2.2.3 (BLP with codewords). Below, we discuss multi-lateral security policies which are more suitable for many usage scenarios and group structures. We start with a multi-lateral policy for confidentiality (the Chinese Wall policy) and one for integrity (the Clark-Wilson policy) before considering other multi-lateral policies.

2.2.1 CHINESE WALL

Chinese Wall[3] is a multi-lateral policy for protecting confidentiality [4]. It is used in many companies whose customers may be competitors of each other, e.g., law firms, advertising agencies and accountant companies, etc. It consists of rules enforced within a company to prevent *conflict-of-interest* (COI) in serving the needs of customers.

Table 2.4 summarizes the Chinese Wall policy. The key idea in the Chinese Wall policy is to divide customers' data-sets into conflict-of-interest (COI) classes. Then, an employee of the company may have access to the *company data-set* (CD) of only one company in a given COI class. So, while the employee may initially have some freedom to choose which company in a COI class to work for, once selected, he may not access any information of another company in that COI class. Furthermore, even after he stops working on a given company's case, he still cannot have access to any other company's data-set in that COI class, for a period of time, set by the company and the circumstances. This is called the *Prior Read* data-sets (PR), and is required since the employee can still remember information from a competitor company's data-set that he has recently worked on. A typical expression of the Chinese Wall rule for a law firm is as follows:

---

[3] The origin of the name is unclear, but an educated guess is that when throwing up a virtual wall between two groups in an organization, the highest and largest physical wall known is the Great Wall of China.

"A partner who has worked recently for one company in a business sector may not have access to the papers of any other company in that sector, for some period of time."

Chinese Wall is a mix of free choice (often called *Discretionary Access Control, DAC*) and *Mandatory Access Control (MAC)*, since a partner is initially free to choose the company in a COI class to work for. It is MAC because once this is selected, the partner must not be allowed to access the data-sets of any other companies in this COI class.

In practice, Chinese Wall is often implemented manually, rather than with automated controls.

The rules for the Chinese Wall policy can be expressed in a similar fashion to those for the BLP security policy, as shown in Table 2.4. The Simple Security policy for Chinese Wall states that a subject can have access to only one dataset in one COI class, except for sanitized objects, which are publicly released objects.

Table 2.4: Chinese Wall rules

Chinese Wall Simple Security policy: A subject S can read an object O iff any of the following holds:
1.   S has already accessed an object in CD(O)
2.   COI(O) is not the same as the COIs of the objects in PR(S)
3.   O is a sanitized object (i.e., publicly released)

Chinese Wall *-property: A subject S can write an object O iff both of the following conditions hold:
1.   Simple Security policy allows S to read O
2.   If S can read unsanitized objects O', S is not allowed to write O unless CD(O) = CD(O')

The Chinese Wall *-property says that even if O1 and O2 are from different COI classes X and Y, respectively, a subject Tom cannot read from O1 and write to O2. This is because another subject Joan could also have access to O2 in COI Y while having access to O3 which belongs to a different company in COI X. If Tom reads from O1 and writes confidential information from O1 to O2, he can illegitimately pass information from O1 to Joan, who is not allowed to access O1 in COI X since she accesses O3, which belongs to competitor company, in COI X. Here, Tom is analogous to the corrupted general in the BLP example given earlier.

Chinese Wall introduces the new concepts of Conflict-Of-Interest (COI) classes, and the Time Element (to deal with human memory or the time period for which protected data remains "current"). One COI class does not "dominate" another, unlike in a hierarchical MLS system. Rather, all COI classes are considered peers, in terms of confidentiality protection.

Table 2.5:   Comparing BLP with Chinese Wall security policy

BLP	Chinese Wall
Protect Confidentiality	Protect Confidentiality
Multi-Level Security (MLS) Policy	Multi-Lateral Security Policy
Has labels	No labels (but has COI classes)
No time element	Has time element (notion of past accesses)
No initial freedom of choice	Initial freedom for subject S to choose which dataset in a COI to access
Mandatory Access Control (MAC) policy	MAC and DAC (Discretionary Access Control) policy
BLP cannot emulate Chinese Wall	Chinese Wall can emulate BLP

Table 2.5 compares the Chinese Wall policy with the BLP policy, since both are policies for protecting confidentiality. BLP requires pre-labeling (also called classification) of objects, and pre-clearance of subjects. Chinese Wall does not require this. Chinese Wall allows some initial freedom of choice and introduces the time element for past accesses of datasets—neither of these concepts are available in BLP. Hence, while BLP can capture the state of a Chinese Wall policy at any given time, it cannot capture its changes over time. Hence BLP cannot faithfully emulate Chinese Wall, but Chinese Wall can emulate BLP. The interested reader can work out how a Chinese Wall policy can emulate the BLP policy, and explain why BLP cannot emulate the Chinese Wall policy.

2.2.2   CLARK-WILSON

The Clark-Wilson policy is for protecting the integrity of data in a multi-lateral environment [5], where no dataset "dominates" another in a hierarchical fashion. It captures, in a formal model, the security policies used in banks, even before computers became ubiquitous. The key ideas are to protect the integrity of data, to protect the integrity of the transactions on the data, and to enforce separation of duty between people who are allowed to operate on data and those whose job is to verify the integrity of the data.

Its first feature is to protect the integrity of data. For integrity, data is said to be consistent if it satisfies certain properties or invariants. Hence, before and after a transaction, the consistency properties must hold. They are checked by Integrity Verification Procedures (IVPs).

Its second feature is to guarantee the integrity of the transactions on protected data. There are pre-deployment and on-going checks to guard against insider attacks. The Clark Wilson policy protects against insider attacks by maintaining *separation of duty*: a person authorized to perform a transaction on a data-set may not also perform integrity verification of the data-set, and vice versa. Implementer and certifier must be different people.

Transactions are used as basic operations in the system. A well-formed transaction is a series of operations that takes the system from a consistent state into another consistent state. While an operation may leave the state in an inconsistent state, the series of operations forming a well-formed transaction must preserve consistency. A transaction must be performed atomically, i.e., the transaction must either complete or the system must be rolled back to a state as if no operation in the partially completed transaction occurred.

Clark Wilson policy consists of two types of procedures: Transformation Procedures (TPs) and Integrity Validation Procedures (IVPs). A TP must be a well-formed transacion. Protected data items are called Certified Data Items (CDIs).

A certified relation is a 2-tuple (TP_i, CDI_j) which associates a TP_i with a set of protected data CDI_j. Other TPs, even if certified, may not operate on this data.

An allowed relation is a 3-tuple $(User_k, TP_i, CDI_j)$ which associates a $User_k$ with a certified relation. This implies that user authentication must be performed before a transaction can be performed on certified data in the Clark-Wilson policy. This 3-tuple can be regarded as defining an element of an access control matrix (described later). The enforcement rules for Transformation Procedures are defined in Table 2.6. Rules 1-3 have already been described above. Table 2.6 also gives the certification rules for Clark-Wilson. The terms "validity," "consistency," and "integrity" are used synonymously. Rule 2 merely states that a TP must take the system from one valid state to another valid state. Rule 3 says that Certifiers of a TP cannot execute that TP, and vice versa (the "separation of duty" rule). Rule 4 requires an audit log. Rule 5 deals with transforming uncertified data into certified data, via a TP.

Table 2.6: Clark-Wilson rules

Enforcement Rules
1. A CDI can only be changed by a TP.
2. A user must be associated with a TP and a CDI.
3. The system must authenticate a user attempting to execute a TP.
4. Only a certifier (e.g., security officer) of a TP can change the authorization list for that TP.
Certification Rules
1. System must have an IVP for verifying the validity of any CDI.
2. The application of any TP to any CDI must maintain its validity.
3. Allowed relations must maintain the principle of separation of duty.
4. Each application of a TP must include an append to an audit log (which must itself be a CDI) with sufficient information to enable the re-construction of the TP.
5. Any TP that takes un-certified data items (UDI) as input must perform only valid (or no) transformations on it and either reject the UDI or turn it into a CDI.

Table 2.7 compares Clark Wilson with Biba, since both support integrity protection. A key difference is that Biba has no certification rules. In Biba, the system assumes that trusted subjects exist to ensure that the Biba rules are enforced. There are no checks on what a trusted subject does. In Clark Wilson, a TP is required to upgrade an entity, and the TP must have previously been certified (by a security officer, for example). Since Biba does not have some of the Clark Wilson features, it cannot emulate Clark Wilson, but Clark Wilson can emulate Biba. The interested reader can work out the mapping of how Clark Wilson can emulate Biba.

Table 2.7: Comparing Clark-Wilson with Biba security policy

Biba	Clark Wilson
Protect Integrity	Protect Integrity
Multi-Level Security (MLS) Policy	Multi-Lateral Security Policy
Has labels (TS, S, C, U) or just (Hi, Lo)	Has labels (CDI=Hi, UDI = Lo)
No certification rules	Has certification rules and Integrity Verification Procedures (IVPs)
No separation of duty	Implements principle of separation of duty between certifiers and implementers
Biba cannot emulate Clark Wilson	Clark Wilson can emulate Biba

2.2.3 BLP WITH CODEWORDS

Most implementations of MLS policies also have a multi-lateral component. We discuss one variant known as *BLP with codewords*.

Giving access to all documents classified at an MLS security level is probably more access than desirable in most cases. Does someone with Top Secret clearance really need to have access to all Top Secret documents? The answer is "no", and BLP with Codewords was created to create multi-lateral compartments within a security level, to implement the concept of "need to know".

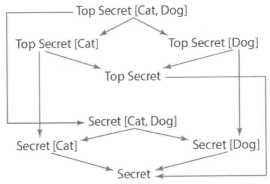

Figure 2.3: BLP with codewords (figure from [7]).

Codewords are used to label disjoint compartments containing documents classified at a given security level *and* codeword. Subjects are also cleared for access to codewords.

Figure 2.3 shows an example of BLP with codewords. An arrow from node A to node B indicates a dominance relationship between these two classes of documents (A ≥ B). Two codewords "Cat" and "Dog" are created for both the TS and S security levels. A subject with clearance TS and codeword Cat can read all TS and S documents with the codeword Cat, and all other TS, S, C and U documents without a codeword. Since he does not have codeword Dog, he may not read TS (Dog) or S (Dog) documents, even though he has TS clearance. He also cannot read TS (Cat, Dog) since he is not cleared for the codeword Dog. Note that dominance (arrow) is defined between some nodes, and not between other nodes. Where dominance relationships exist, the BLP read and write rules apply. If no dominance relationship exists, no access is allowed. The structure in Figure 2.3 resembles a *lattice*, a mathematical structure, and this security policy is also called a *lattice model*.

2.2.4 ELECTRONIC MEDICAL RECORDS

Real-world policies may be more complicated than one of the models discussed above. We illustrate with a policy for online medical records, proposed some time ago for the British Medical Association (BMA). It has a multi-lateral policy with some aspects of Multi-Level Security embedded in it. Table 2.8 gives a very condensed summary of the BMA policy. Full details can be found in[6]. The BMA policy consists of nine principles. It defines an Access Control List (ACL) for each medical record, which specifies who may read or append (not arbitrarily modify) the record for a given patient (#1). Someone must be on the ACL for this record to open it (#2). It specifies that one doctor may be the only one who can change the ACL (#3), and that the patient must be notified unless it is an emergency (#4). Furthermore, no one—not even the primary doctor who can change the ACL nor the patient, can delete a medical record until a given period of time has passed (#5). To help with attribution in case of a security or privacy breach, an audit trail must be kept (#6). For writing, a BLP rule is used (#7)—this is a "no write down" rule since fewer people can read B (hence B must be classified at a higher confidentiality level) than can read A. The patient must be notified (and presumably his consent must be obtained) before his medical data is made accessible to some entity doing a research study or statistical survey (#8). Finally, any computer handling medical records should have a Trusted Computing Base (TCB) that enforces this BMA policy. This was said to be the hardest aspect of the BMA policy to achieve, and is, in fact, still not achievable by commonly used computer systems.

Table 2.8: BMA policy for medical records

1. Access control: each record has an ACL for who may read or append
2. Record opening: patient, doctor, consulting doctor must be on ACL
3. ACL Control: only one of clinicians on ACL may alter ACL (responsible clinician)
4. Consent and notification: Responsible clinician must notify patient of accesses, ACL changes, ACL responsibility transfer, except in emergencies
5. Persistence: No one can delete information until appropriate time period has expired
6. Attribution: Mark all accesses to clinical record; audit trail for all deletions
7. Information flow: Information derived from record A may be appended to record B iff B's ACL is contained in A's
8. Aggregation control: measures to prevent aggregation of personal health info, e.g., patients must be specially notified if person to be added to their ACL already has access to a large number of records
9. Trusted computing base: computer systems handling personal health information must have a subsystem that enforces above principles effectively, subject to evaluation by independent experts

We have discussed different security policy models—both multi-level security and multi-lateral security—in this chapter. In the next chapter, we see some ways security policies can be enforced by systems software or hardware.

CHAPTER 3

Access Control

Security Policies, discussed in the previous chapter, are enforced to control access to protected information. Access control consists of two parts: Authentication and Authorization. Authentication mechanisms identify who the subject is. Authorization mechanisms determine what access the subject is allowed to the object.

3.1 AUTHENTICATION

Authentication can be done by various means, and in fact is the most common aspect of computer security known to users. A user performs a "log in" with his/her username and password to authenticate himself/herself to the system. Here the password is used for user authentication.

Traditionally, authentication has been done by one of the following three methods, shown in Table 3.1. Multi-factor authentication uses more than one mechanism to authenticate a user.

Table 3.1: Traditional authentication mechanisms

Authentication based on one or more of:
• What you know
• What you are
• What you have

3.1.1 PASSWORDS AND PASSPHRASES

An example of "what you know" is your password or passphrase. Random passwords are better against password cracking attempts, however they are hard for human users to remember. One way that has been shown to be as good as random passwords, and easy for a human to remember, is to turn a secret passphrase into a password. For example, the passphrase, "We go to Maine every summer for hiking" can be turned into the password "wg2m#Sfh". This uses the first letter of each word of the passphrase, substituting numbers, upper case letters or symbols for some of the letters. This looks like a random password, which will not be found in any dictionary of common passwords. Password dictionaries list the most common passwords in decreasing order of frequency. They are used in *dictionary attacks* to crack passwords.

3.1.2 BIOMETRICS

An example of "what you are" is a biometric. One of the oldest biometrics used before computers became ubiquitous is handwriting, as used in signatures. Fingerprinting, face recognition, voice recognition, hand recognition and iris scans are other biometrics that have been used. Here, one has to be concerned with the False Accept Rate (FAR) versus the False Reject Rate (FRR), discussed in the next section. Iris scan, done properly, is the most accurate biometric. However, it is not as commonly used as some of the less accurate biometrics because of its expense, and the public's feeling that it may be intrusive or even harmful to scan one's eye so often at close quarters.

3.1.3 PRIVATE KEYS AND SECURITY TOKENS

An example of "what you have" is a security token, or a private key used in public key cryptography, discussed in more detail in a later chapter. In public-key cryptography, keys come in matched pairs: (public key, private key) for each user, entity, computer or subject. The private key must be accessible only to the subject and represents his/her/its digital identity in cyberspace.

3.1.4 FALSE NEGATIVES AND FALSE POSITIVES

In biometrics, the algorithms used to recognize a person by his biometric is probabilistic, and some errors can occur. A *False Accept* is when an imposter is authenticated as a legitimate user. The *False Accept Rate* (FAR) is also called the *fraud rate* (see Table 3.2). A False Reject is when a legitimate user is denied access. The *False Reject Rate* (FRR) is also called the *insult rate*. In most biometrics, tweaking the biometric system to lower the FAR will result in increasing the FRR, and vice versa. Banks are often willing to increase the fraud rate slightly so as to reduce the insult rate to customers, for fear the customers will go to competitive banks. The *Equal Error Rate*, EER, is when the FAR is equal to the FRR.

False Accepts are also called *False Negatives*, because the system did not detect a security breach (an imposter or intruder)—it did not raise an alarm (negative) when it should have. False Rejects are also called *False Positives*, because the system detected a security breach (an imposter or intruder) erroneously—it raised an alarm (positive) when it should *not* have. While the goal of a security mechanism is to prevent security breaches (and hence prevent false negatives from slipping through), in practice, false positives (which raise annoying false alarms) can be more problematic. When too many false alarms are raised, users will try to turn off the security mechanism, or find ways to bypass it, or completely ignore it. The system may even be unusable if the false positive rate is high, and deployment will be very limited.

Table 3.2: False positives and false negatives

False Negative (FN)	False Positive (FP)
False Accept Rate (FAR)	False Reject Rate (FRR)
Fraud Rate	Insult Rate

Understanding the False Negative Rate (equivalently the False Accept Rate) and the False Positive Rate (equivalently the False Reject Rate) is very important in the design of all security mechanisms, not just for biometrics or authentication systems. In most security mechanisms, things are not strictly "black and white", hence there will be errors made in classifying something as a security attack or not. We need to understand the tradeoff between absolute, guaranteed security (no false negatives) versus usable security (low false positives).

3.2   AUTHORIZATION

For computer architects used to designing general-purpose computers, we naturally want to be able to implement computers that can enforce all possible security policies—but as you can see even from looking at just a few relatively simple security policy models, this is not an easy task. For example, there are Mandatory Access Control (MAC) policies, where the system decides who gets access to what and users have no choice, and there are Discretionary Access Control (DAC) policies, where the user decides who gets access to objects he owns or controls. Then, there are policies which combine aspects of both MAC and DAC, or cannot be described as either MAC or DAC.

Table 3.3 shows an example of an Access Control Matrix (ACM) with subjects as rows and objects as columns. Although this ACM has only the actions Read (R) and Write (W), in general, entries can also indicate other allowed actions including Execute (X), Append (A), Delegate (D), etc. ACMs can get very large as the number of subjects and objects increase. A subject can also be a program, not necessarily a person. A program or a person could also be an "object" to be protected, since this is a resource.

Table 3.3: An Access Control Matrix (ACM)

	A's grade in X	A's grade in Y	A's transcript	B's grade in X	B's grade in Y	B's transcript
Student A	R	R	R	-	-	-
Student B	-	-	-	R	R	R
Professor of class X	R,W	-	-	R,W	-	-
Professor of class Y	-	R,W	-	-	R,W	-
Registrar	R	R	R	R	R	R

An Access Control Matrix can also be stored as columns, or as rows. As columns, these are called Access Control Lists (ACLs), where an ACL is associated with each object. An ACL defines who may have what access to that object. As rows, they are called Capability lists (c-lists) associated with each subject. A subject has a list of capabilities, which define what types of access that subject has to different objects. Hence, a subject (which can be a program) cannot even access an object unless it has the capability for that object.

Capability-based machines carry this further to the point that capabilities replace memory addresses for accessing objects. If a subject (e.g., a program or person) does not have the capability for that object, it cannot even retrieve the object. Although no capability-based computer has achieved widespread deployment, this is mainly due to performance reasons. Nevertheless, there are many advocates for capability machines in the security community.

Capability machines viewed as "tagged architectures," can be seen to be very useful for security, power-management, etc. Computer architects who like the idea of capabilities (rather than memory addresses) to access objects, or tags on data for whatever purpose, just have to figure out how to build a very high-performance, efficient and low-power capability machine! Indeed, there seems to be a resurgence of interest in tagged architectures and/or capability-based architectures. Non-security related mechanisms, such as speculation and transactional memory, are also providing motivation for tagged architectures.

Most common operating systems, like Windows and Linux, use ACLs associated with the objects (files). ACLs are easier to implement, and to change access rights for a given object. C-lists may be more convenient if a subject leaves a company—his entire c-list can be deleted, rather than searching through all the ACLs for the objects.

Most of the security policy models described in the previous chapter can be described eventually by an Access Control Matrix (ACM), if we allow more complicated entries in it. For example, for the Clark Wilson policy, we have to put TPs and IVPs (Transformation Procedures and Integrity Verification Procedures) in the ACM entries. For the Chinese Wall policy, some of these entries have to be conditioned on the Prior Read (PR) set of that individual, which is a separate data structure from the ACM. Similarly, the period of time after which a subject has stopped accessing a CD in a COI and when he is allowed to access a different CD in that COI is a separate procedure that updates the ACM representing a Chinese Wall policy.

Table 3.4: Some types of access control

Name	Type of Access Control	Access Control determined by:
MAC	Mandatory Access Control	system
DAC	Discretionary Access Control	user
RBAC	Role-Based Access Control	role
ORCON	Originator-Controlled Access Control	originator (or creator) of document

Table 3.4 summarizes some different types of access control. Mandatory Access Control (MAC) is determined by the system. The MLS policies are MAC policies, including BLP and Biba. Chinese Wall has elements of both DAC and MAC. For example, a subject can initally choose which CD (set of documents) in a Conflict of Interest (COI) class to access if this is the first time he is accessing any document in that COI class—this is DAC. However, once he has accessed a document in a particulat CD in a COI class, he cannot access any other CD in that COI class—this is the MAC aspect.

In RBAC [11], access is given to roles rather than to individual users. A user must not only be authenticated, but his current role must be determined. For example, in an Access Control Matrix, a role can be listed in a row, such as a "system administrator", rather than an individual. If Tom Smith is acting in his role as a system administrator, he may be allowed access to all files for backup purposes. However, if he is in his role as a soccer dad (i.e., not a system administrator), he may not have access to other users' files, including a competitor team's "play strategies" document. If Jane Chen is also authenticated as a system administrator, she will also have the rights of that role.

In ORCON [12, 13], neither the system nor the user determines the access control rules, but rather the originator of the document determines who may access this document under what conditions. This is neither a DAC nor MAC policy, or can be considered a bit of both. ORCON is very difficult to enforce across a distributed system, and is often called the "holy grail" of access control policies. Note that Digital Rights Management (DRM) would be a solved problem if ORCON can be reliably enforced. Recent work at implementing an ORCON-like policy, with new hardware support, can be found in [14, 15].

Access Control Matrices, Access Control Lists and Capability-lists and their enforcement mechanisms can be used as mechanisms for implementing various security policies. They often need to be supplemented by other mechanisms for updating these ACMs, ACLs and C-lists. These structures and the procedures that operate on them need to be in the Trusted Computing Base in order for the security policies they implement to be enforced.

There are also other mechanisms for implementing security policies, generally called Policy Engines, which evaluate arbitrary security policies expressed in policy languages, to decide whether to allow or deny access to an object by a subject.

CHAPTER   4

Cryptography for Confidentiality and Integrity

Cryptography provides us with excellent tools to enhance the confidentiality and integrity of information in computer architectures. It can be used to provide information security during transmission, computing and storage. In this and the next chapter, we discuss three basic cryptographic methods:

- symmetric-key ciphers for confidentiality protection,

- cryptographic hash functions for integrity protection, and

- public-key ciphers for establishing a longer-term cyber identity, e.g., for authentication (next chapter).

We also give examples of how these cryptographic techniques can be used in *security-aware processors* to protect keys and security policies, which then protect other objects cryptographically, for confidentiality and integrity. Cryptographic methods can also be used to provide a secure execution environment for trusted software, and protect both memory and storage.

4.1   SYMMETRIC KEY CIPHERS

We first present basic terminology and components for encryption and decryption. Figure 4.1 shows a generic cryptosystem. The original message or information to be encrypted is called the *plaintext*. An encryption function takes the plaintext, together with a key, and produces the *ciphertext*. The ciphertext is like gibberish and is unintelligible, as long as a strong cipher is used for the encryption and the key is kept secret, i.e., inaccessible to an adversary. Hence, the ciphertext can be safely distributed, e.g., transmitted over public networks, or stored in ordinary (unprotected) storage devices. For strong ciphers, the ciphertext can only be decrypted if the key is available, by a matching decryption function, yielding the original plaintext.

In a symmetric-key cipher, the same secret key is used for encryption and decryption. (This statement is not as obvious as it may seem. In the next chapter, we discuss public-key ciphers, where one key is used for encryption, another for decryption.)

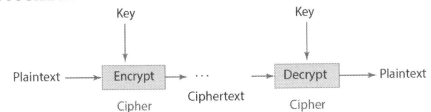

Figure 4.1:   Components in a cryptosystem.

One strategy for protecting the confidentiality of some information is to allow encrypted data, i.e., ciphertext, to be freely distributed, but restrict access to the plaintext and the key to authorized users only. I will call this *cryptographic access control*.

Symmetric-key encryption is very useful for *bulk encryption*, i.e., encrypting a large amount of data, and hence protecting its confidentiality by keeping the encryption key secret. When the key is used by an authorized party for decrypting the ciphertext, the plaintext must be accessed in a *secure environment*, to preserve its confidentiality.

There are two main types of symmetric-key ciphers: block ciphers and stream ciphers. We first look at some basic mechanisms behind block ciphers (e.g., substitutions and permutations) and stream ciphers (e.g., one-time pad). We then discuss the basic structure of stream ciphers and block ciphers, giving some important examples like A5/1, DES, 3DES and AES.

4.1.1   SUBSTITUTION AND PERMUTATION CIPHERS

Symmetric-key ciphers use a combination of *confusion* and *diffusion* operations [16]. Simple ciphers often use substitutions, via table-lookups, as an example of a confusion operation, and permutations (or transpositions), as an example of a diffusion operation.

A simple substitution cipher is Caesar's cipher, one of the earliest ciphers. For each plaintext letter, this substitutes a letter that is three letters to the right in alphabetic order, to get the ciphertext letter. Here, the key is 3 and the encryption operation is rotation of the alphabet. For this simple substitution cipher, it is not even necessary to look up a table to do the substitution, since the ciphertext can just be computed as

$$C_i = (P_i + 3) \bmod 26, \text{ for } i = 1, 2, \ldots, n,$$

where each letter is given a number from 0 to 25 according to its alphabetical order, and n is the number of letters in the plaintext.

Instead of 3, the key can be any integer from 1 to 26. Also, the operation need not be rotation, but can be any permutation of the 26 letters of the alphabet, thus increasing the key space from 26 to 26! possible keys, where $26! = 26*25*24*\ldots*2*1$, which is approximately 2^{88} different keys.

Another common operation used in ciphers is permutation (also called transpositions or re-arrangements) of the plaintext. The permutation can be done in one or more dimensions. For example, in a two-dimensional transposition cipher, the plaintext letters can be put into an mxn matrix, from left to right, top to bottom. The rows and columns can then be permuted, to give the ciphertext. The key for decryption is the size of the matrix (m, n), the permutation of the rows and the permutation of the columns. For example, if m=5 rows, the permutation of the rows can be expressed as a cycle, e.g., (4,3,5,1,2). Similarly, if n=7 for the columns, the permutation of the columns can be expresses as a cycle, e.g., (2,7,1,3,6,5,4).

In general, a cipher composed of only permutation operations is not as secure as one with substitutions as well, and most ciphers involve some elements of substitutions and permutations.

4.1.2   ONE TIME PAD

A One Time Pad (OTP) is one of the simplest ciphers, involving just an exclusive-OR of each plaintext bit with a key bit to get a ciphertext bit:

$$C_i = P_i \text{ XOR } K_i \text{, for i = 1, 2, ..., n,} \tag{1}$$

where C_i is the ciphertext bit, P_i is the plaintext bit, K_i is the key bit, and n is the number of bits in the plaintext.

The idea is that the key is a random string (the One Time Pad), where each key bit is only used "one time", and never reused.

This is a provably secure cipher if the key has the following properties:

• is random (i.e., all possible OTPs are equally likely),

• is as long as the plaintext, and

• is known only to the sender and the receiver.

This information-theoretic security can be defined as:

$$\text{Prob}\{ P = i \mid C = j\} = \text{Prob}\{ P = i \} \tag{2}$$

However, how can the key pad be generated and transmitted securely to the receiver? If this could be done securely over a public network, then the plaintext could be transmitted securely in the same way!

Another difficulty is that the receiver's key pad must be perfectly synchronized with the sender, otherwise decryption will not yield the same plaintext.

As with other ciphers, an OTP encryption makes no claims about integrity. A different OTP could be used to decrypt the ciphertext, resulting in a different plaintext message, and the receiver would not be able to detect this.

4.1.3   STREAM CIPHERS

Stream ciphers encrypt plaintext a bit at a time, or a byte at a time. They are very suitable for bit-serial or byte-serial communications, where the data or message to be encrypted is sent out serially and received serially.

Stream ciphers try to capitalize on the efficiency of the OTP using only an XOR operation to produce the ciphertext bit (or byte). Although it is impractical to try to produce a random key pad that is as long as the plaintext to be encrypted, it is possible to generate a pseudo-random sequence of bits with a very long period, using Linear Feedback Shift Registers (LFSRs). A physically random seed can be used to initialize the LFSRs. Other ways of extending the random key pad are also possible.

Example of a stream cipher: A5/1

Figure 4.2 shows an example of a stream cipher, the A5/1, used to encrypt GSM voice messages [6, 7]. The 64-bit key is used to initialize the three LFSRs which are 19, 22 and 23 bits long, respectively. At each cycle, the LFSRs step, or not, depending on the values of their three middle bits, (x_8, y_{10}, z_{10}). If x_8 = majority (x_8, y_{10}, z_{10}), then the x register steps, i.e., it shifts right by one bit position. Also, the XOR of the selected bits from the x register is performed with the result bit written to the leftmost bit of the x register. If x_8 differs from the majority (x_8, y_{10}, z_{10}), then the x register contents do not change. Similarly, if y_{10} = majority (x_8, y_{10}, z_{10}), then the y register steps, else its contents do not change. Similarly, for the z register. The rightmost bits of the three LFSRs are then XOR'ed together to give the next bit of the key pad.

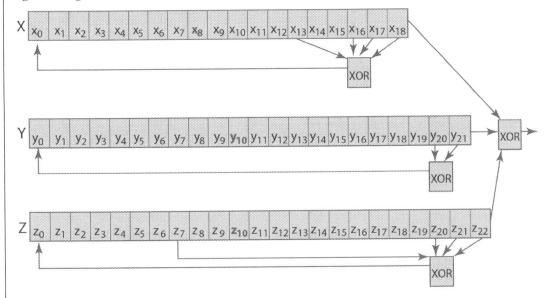

Figure 4.2: Stream cipher, A5/1, uses three LFSRs to generate the key pad.

Although A5/1 has been broken [34, 35], it was still used for a long time in GSM cellphones. It illustrates how hardware-efficient a stream cipher can be, especially if the input comes in one bit at a time. If the plaintext comes in k bits at a time, the key pad can be generated at least k bits ahead of time, so that it is ready when needed for either encryption or decryption; it will then take only one cycle to XOR k plaintext bits with k key pad bits.

4.1.4 BLOCK CIPHERS

Block ciphers divide the plaintext into non-overlapping, fixed-length blocks, and encode each plaintext block into a ciphertext block of the same length. Figure 4.3 shows the structure of a typical block cipher, consisting of n rounds of computation, with a possible prologue in front, and a possible epilogue at the end. The n rounds are usually identical, like iterations of a loop, but each round uses the block generated from the previous round and a different round key as inputs. The round keys are generated from the secret key, and need only be done once for encrypting many blocks of plaintext with the same key. (Sometimes there are two types of rounds: even rounds and odd rounds, and sometimes the last round may be different from previous rounds.)

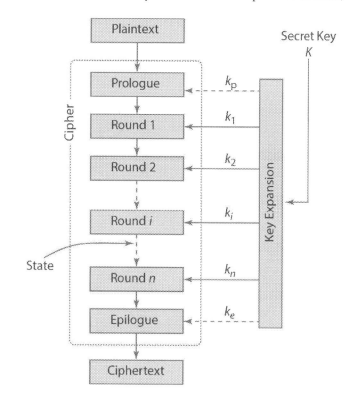

Figure 4.3: Structure of a block cipher.

A cipher is defined by its round function, its block size, its key size and its number of rounds. Assuming all the rounds are the same, the cipher's minimum latency is generally (n*d+c) cycles, if it has n rounds and each round can be done in d cycles, and c cycles are taken by the prologue and epilogue.

Example: DES and Triple DES

The Data Encryption Standard (DES) was the NIST standard for encryption and decryption [17] for over two decades, before it was replaced by the Advanced Encryption Standard (AES) [18]. It is a Feistal cipher, which has the unique characteristic that the same circuit can be used for encryption or decryption, with the round keys used in reverse order.

A Fiestal cipher is a rather beautiful mathematical construct where the input block to each round of the cipher is divided into two halves: L and R. The right half of the input of each stage, e.g., R_{i-1} in Figure 4.4, becomes the left half input of the next stage. The left half of each stage, viz., L_{i-1}, is XOR'ed with a function f of R_{i-1} and the round key, K_i, to give the right half of the next stage.

The same circuit can be used for both encryption and decryption if the order of the subkeys used as round keys is reversed. This is equivalent to deriving L_{i-1} and R_{i-1} from L_i and R_i in Figure 4.4, as follows: R_{i-1} is derived directly from L_i. Then, S_i is derived by computing $f(R_{i-1}, K_i)$ and this can be XOR'ed with R_i to give L_{i-1}. Note that the function f does not have to be invertible for decryption to work!

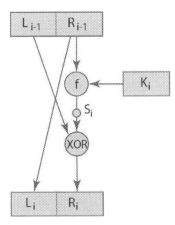

Figure 4.4: Feistal cipher: structure of each round.

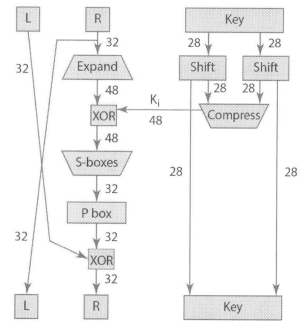

Figure 4.5: One round of DES.

Figure 4.5 shows one round of DES encryption on the left, where the Feistel structure is clearly seen. In DES, the block size is 64 bits and the key size is 56 bits (with 8 bits of parity). The function f consists of an expansion of the right half of the input to 48 bits, an XOR with the round key (generated by the circuit on the right), some substitutions (denoted by S-box) and a permutation (denoted by P-box). Round keys can be generated once and used for the encryption (or decryption) of many plaintext (or ciphertext) blocks.

Triple DES (3DES) was invented when 56-bit DES was broken. It involved encryption with one key, decryption with a second key and encryption with a third key (which was the first key), giving the effect of a 112-bit key:

$$C = E_{K1} (D_{K2} (E_{K1} (P))) \qquad (3)$$

where E_K and D_K refer to Encryption and Decryption, respectively, with key K.

At the time, doubling the key size seemed more than sufficient—tripling it was not necessary. The encryption-decryption-encryption sequence of 3DES was chosen, so that 3DES encryption engines can be compatible with DES, by just replacing K2 with K1. Many systems still use 3DES encryption, but DES is used less often these days.

Advanced Encryption Standard, AES

A cipher, Rijndael [20], won the competition for the Advanced Encryption Standard (AES) sponsored by NIST. It is now known as the AES cipher, the new standard for symmetric-key encryption and decryption [18]. A very good animation of AES encryption is given in [19].

AES has 128-bit blocks with three possible key sizes: 128 bits, 192 bits and 256 bits. Depending on the key size, AES performs 10, 12 or 14 rounds, respectively. Each round of AES consists of four simple operations:

- ByteSub   ; nonlinear layer

- ShiftRow   ; linear mixing layer

- MixColumn   ; nonlinear layer

- AddRoundKey   ; key addition layer

Consider AES with 128 bit keys and ten rounds. Each 128-bit block of plaintext is arranged as a 4x4 matrix of 16 bytes. The ByteSub operation substitutes each byte of the plaintext with a byte of the AES table (where all entries are known constants). There are four AES tables, each with 256 entries. The ShiftRow operation rotates each of the four rows left by 0, 1, 2 and 3 bytes, respectively. MixColumn does a permutation operation on the columns, using a multiplication of each column of the state by a 4x4 matrix (of constants) (Note that in software cipher implementations, permutation of bytes in a column is much harder than permutation of bytes in a row. The latter fit in a register, but the former has bytes coming from, and going to, four different registers.) AddRoundKey XORs each byte of the intermediate result matrix with the key matrix. The last AES round does not have the MixColumn step.

In AES decryption, each round consists of the inverse of each of the four encryption steps. Hence, unlike DES, AES requires separate circuits for encryption versus decryption.

4.1.5   PROCESSOR ENHANCEMENTS FOR CRYPTO

If cryptographic processing is to be used extensively, we want it to be very fast, and to incur very little overhead. Ideally, it should incur no overhead. Toward this end, processor designers need to understand what ciphers do and hence how to accelerate them. This is why we have described cipher structures and a few ciphers including AES. Ciphers—there are thousands of these—can be implemented in software or in hardware. Since multiple ciphers typically need to be implemented, software implementations are more flexible, if we can make these very fast.[4] We show two examples: one that is cipher-specific and another that is more general purpose.

---

[4]   Today, adding multiple hardware crypto accelerators into processor chips has lower opportunity costs, especially considering that accelerators may actually save power. However, there are still only a finite number of accelerators one can put in hardware on a chip.

Intel has introduced six new special-purpose SSE instructions to speed up AES processing in software, called AES-NI [21]. One instruction does one round of AES encryption, a second instruction does the final round AES encryption. A third instruction does one round of AES decryption, and a fourth instruction does the final round of AES decryption. Finally two new instructions help speed up AES key generation.

Instead of these AES-specific instructions, it is also possible to do fast software AES with new general purpose instructions [22]. Lee proposes two general-purpose instructions that not only accelerate AES, but also accelerate other ciphers and non-cryptographic algorithms:

- a Parallel Table Lookup instruction (**Pread**), and

- a **byte-permute** instruction

The **Pread** instruction behaves like a 2-read 1-write computation operation, but does two reads of 8 small scratchpad memories in parallel, combining the results with a combinatorial function into one result for the destination register. One of the operands to the **Pread** instruction contains the indices for the parallel table lookups. The second operand is a mask which can be applied to the table lookup results together with the combinatorial function.

The **byte_permute** instruction enables re-ordering of the bytes in a register.

These two instructions enable each of the first nine rounds of AES to be done in only two cycles (one cycle for each instruction), and the last round can be done in only three cycles, with a total of 22 cycles per block for encryption (with one cycle initialization). This achieves 128-bit AES at 1.38 cycles per byte, which is faster than the special-purpose Intel AES-NI instructions when they each took six cycles to execute. Tradeoffs may be in area, which has not been compared.

The key idea is to combine the AES ByteSub and MixColumn operations into a single lookup of a larger table, and fold the fourth step (XOR with round key) into a single **Pread** instruction [22]. Then, the Shift Row operation is achieved by reordering the bytes in the source register using the **byte_permute** operation; these bytes are used as indices to look up the various tables, for the next round. Thus each AES round is done by only two instructions (**Pread**, **byte_permute**) in two cycles. The mask in the **Pread** instruction allows the last AES round to be done in only three cycles.

While cryptographic processing may be important enough in the future that it may warrant hardware AES implementation, the above shows that if new Instruction Set Architecture (ISA) is allowed, software crypto processing can be made almost as fast as hardware implementations—and can even be done with general-purpose instructions rather than only with cipher-specific instructions like [21].

4.1.6   CIPHER MODES OF OPERATION

It is very important to understand that encrypting each block separately (called Electronic Code Book, ECB, mode) is not sufficient. This is because identical plaintext blocks will give identical ciphertext blocks—hence, giving away information. Furthermore, cut-and-paste attacks are possible. For example, in a form letter, an attacker can know where the sender and recipient names are, or where dollar amounts are, and can replace them with other names and amounts, by merely substituting or re-ordering the ciphertext blocks, even if he cannot decrypt the blocks. To overcome these limitations of ECB mode, other cipher modes of operation are preferred. There are many modes of operation, but we will illustrate with three popular ones: ECB (electronic code book), CBC (cipher block chaining) and CTR (counter mode) as shown in Figure 4.6.

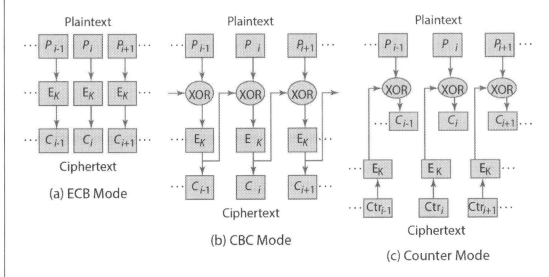

Figure 4.6: Cipher modes of operation: electronic code book (ECB) (a), cipher block chaining (CBC) (b), and counter mode (CTR) (c). E_K denotes Encryption with key K.

The Cipher Block Chaining (CBC) mode XORs the ciphertext of the previous block with the plaintext of the current block, before encrypting the current block (see Figure 4.6 (b)). This way, the ciphertext of identical plaintext blocks will not be the same. While encryption is serialized (e.g., have to encrypt 99 blocks before can encrypt the 100th block), this is not generally a problem, since encryption is usually done serially anyway.

An advantage of CBC mode is that decryption is not serialized, but is "random access". We can decrypt ciphertext block i immediately, then XOR it with ciphertext block (i-1) to get plaintext block i:

$$\text{CBC encryption: } C_i = E(\, C_{i-1} \text{ XOR } P_i \,)$$

$$\text{CBC decryption: } P_i = D(C_i) \text{ XOR } C_{i-1}$$

Counter-mode encryption is another very useful mode. In addition to preventing the ECB problem of identical ciphertext blocks for identical plaintext blocks, counter mode can also reduce the latency of encryption, thus improving performance. In counter-mode encryption, we first seed a counter with an initial value, then encrypt the counter value, which is then just XOR'ed with the plaintext block when it comes, to get the ciphertext block. Decryption is the same, involving just an XOR. It should be clear that the encryption of counters can be done ahead of time, so that the critical-time latency for encryption is just an additional XOR, when the plaintext data is available for encryption.

Likewise, if the counters are encrypted ahead of time, decryption is also just an XOR of the appropriate encrypted counter with the ciphertext block, when the latter arrives. Counter-mode encryption is like a stream cipher where the plaintext and key are two streams of blocks, rather than two streams of bits or bytes. A block is 64 bits for DES, and 128 bits for AES.

$$\text{Counter-mode encryption: } C_i = E(\, Ctr_i \,) \text{ XOR } P_i$$

$$\text{Counter-mode decryption: } P_i = E(Ctr_i \,) \text{ XOR } C_i$$

The difficulty with counter-mode is that the counters for decryption must be remembered (or regenerated) and must be synchronized with those used for the encryption. Many papers in computer architecture conferences propose performance improvements by just using counter-mode encryption and decryption, e.g. [23, 24].

4.1.7   IMPORTANCE OF KEY MANAGEMENT

A key premise of modern cryptography is that the cipher (cryptographic algorithm) itself should not be secret—only the key should be kept secret. This is called *Kerckhoff's Principle*. By making the algorithm known, both white-hat hackers (good guys) and black-hat hackers (bad guys) can attack the cipher, and thus find weaknesses in it. Generally, shortly after making a secret cryptographic algorithm public, we find it broken by someone.

Hence, the most important aspect of using cryptography to provide confidentiality protection is to protect the secret key. There are many ways to do this. One way is to provide, or even generate, the key when it is needed. Then, delete it once it is no longer needed. Another method, when a large number of keys may be involved, is to hierarchically encrypt the keys, keeping the master key protected by hardware.

4.1.8   COMPUTER ARCHITECTURE EXAMPLE: SP

We give an extensive list of papers on "Secure Processors," (in Appendix: Further Readings), which use some aspects of cryptography to protect the confidentiality and/or integrity of some aspects of the hardware (persistent storage, or memory, or registers) or software. Here, we illustrate with a minimalist secure processor: the Secret Protection (SP) architecture [25, 26], which was designed to be as simple as possible, while providing confidentiality for secret or sensitive data.

Since hardware architecture should be used only for the most essential or fundamental aspects of security (functions that are very slow, difficult or impossible for software to achieve), using new hardware to help improve the security of key management is perhaps the most important aspect of hardware-enhanced cryptographic protection.

SP tried to identify the minimal set of *hardware trust anchors* for providing confidentiality. These are new registers, with associated mechanisms, that hold the *roots of trust* for providing important security features, like confidentiality or integrity. Several usage modes of the SP architecture have been proposed, including user-mode SP [25], authority-mode SP [26], sensor-mode SP [27, 28] and embedded-mode SP [29], to test the validity of these hardware trust anchors under very different usage scenarios.

The usage scenario for *User-mode SP* [25] is equivalent to a user, today, storing his confidential information in the Cloud, encrypted with a key that only he has access to. The user accesses this information, stored online, through his SP-enabled computing device. Since there can be an essentially unlimited number of keys used (for different movies, music, work files and personal files) even for a single user, how can these keys be kept securely—using minimal new hardware? The solution proposed in [25] is to encrypt the keys themselves, and have the user provide a master key, called a User_Master_Key, that only he knows. This is temporarily stored for this session in a new protected register, and used to decrypt keys in different key-chains of keys. Hence, only the User_Master_Key has to be securely protected by the hardware. The hierarchically encrypted key-chains can be stored in regular (insecure) storage—and hence any number of keys and key-chains can be stored—using strong cryptography to protect the confidentiality of the keys. Hence, minimal new hardware is added to provide secure storage enabled with hardware cryptography, to store critical secrets like keys and security policies, which can then protect any number of secret, sensitive or proprietary objects or files, using strong symmetric-key encryption.

Another method to enhance the security of cryptographic keys is to generate the keys only when they are needed. Only one root key needs to be securely stored—preferably with hardware protection—and the other keys generated at runtime when needed for encryption or decryption.

When generating new keys from a single key, *key diversification* can be used. For example, a keyed-hash (discussed in the next section) can be used to generate a new key from a *nonce* (a **n**umber used **once**) and one or more constants. In Authority-mode SP [26], key diversification and dynamic key generation is used to generate session keys for cryptographically secured communications channels over the insecure, public networks, and to generate symmetric keys for secure storage of other keys and confidential information.

Secure Execution Environment

It is important to understand that protecting the crypto keys is also not sufficient. One must also protect the decrypted plaintext. To accomplish both key protection and protection of the plaintext, the SP architecture defines trusted software modules (TSMs) as the only software that may access the keys and decrypt the protected information. The SP hardware tries to provide a secure execution environment for the execution of such TSMs, using another hardware trust anchor called the Device_Master_Key. This provides runtime cryptographic protection of the TSM code, the TSM's memory, and the general registers on interrupts.

4.2   CRYPTOGRAPHIC HASH FUNCTIONS

From encryption to protect confidentiality, we now turn to cryptographic hash functions to protect integrity. A cryptographic hash function is like an electronic fingerprint of a message. It takes a message of arbitrary length and compresses it into a short, fixed-length hash value, such that whenever even a bit in the message changes, the resulting hash value will change (see Figure 4.7). A cryptographic hash function is said to "compress" since it generates a fixed size hash value (e.g., 128, 160, 256 or 512 bits, depending on the hash function), from a string of arbitrary length (e.g., a 5 Gigabyte file).

We drew Figure 4.7 to make it look like the block cipher in Figure 4.3. However, note that while the plaintext block is input into a block cipher, a constant, called an Initialization Vector (IV), is input into a hash function. The message to be hashed is divided into blocks (typically much larger blocks than the plaintext blocks in block ciphers). Each message block is input into one hash computation, f, and there are as many repetitions of f as there are message blocks. Each hash computation, f, consists of a fixed number of rounds, typically many more than the fixed number of rounds in a block cipher. Hence, while there are similarities between a hash function and a block cipher, there are also many differences.

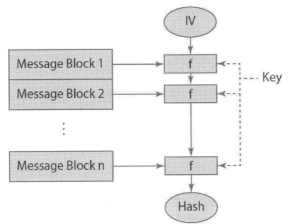

Figure 4.7: Cryptographic Hash function (the dotted lines indicate that the key is optional and is used only for keyed-hash, also called MAC, functions).

Commonly used hash functions are MD5 (Message Digest 5) and SHA (Secure Hash Algorithm). Both have message block sizes of 512 bits (64 bytes), i.e., the message of arbitrary length is partitioned into disjoint 512-bit blocks and input into successive invocations of the hash computation. For MD5, the Initial Vector, IV, and the Hash Output are 128 bits, while for SHA-1, they are 160 bits. We discuss the significance of the length of the hash function later.

4.2.1   PROPERTIES OF CRYPTOGRAPHIC HASH FUNCTIONS

In the following, let M denote an arbitrary message and h(M) denote the hash function of M. A cryptographic hash function has the following properties:

- Compression: $|M| \geq |h(M)|$

- Efficient: Given input x, easy to find h(x)

- One-way: Given y, hard to find x such that $y = h(x)$

- Collision Resistant:

   ○ Given M1, h(M1), it is computationally infeasible to find any M2 such that h(M1) = h(M2)   {weak collision resistance}

   ○ It is computationally infeasible to find any two messages M1 & M2 such that h(M1) = h(M2)   {strong collision resistance}

The hash functions used in software hash tables are not cryptographic hash functions, neither are CRC (Cyclic Redundancy Check) hash functions. They do not satisfy all the properties above; in particular, they do not provide collision resistance.

By *computationally infeasible*, cryptographers use a very huge factor as a safety margin, so it is not a concern that computation power (actually transistors on a chip) doubles every year and a half, as in Moore's Law. Rather, it is more like saying that the expected number of trials needed to break the hash function (by brute force trial and error) would be greater than the number of atoms in the universe. Continuing advances like quantum computing, and advances in number theory, also make it harder to define computational infeasibility.

4.2.2 COLLISION RESISTANCE AND THE BIRTHDAY PARADOX

To illustrate the weak and strong collision properties, the "birthday paradox" analogy is often helpful (see Section 4.3).

This shows that for a hash function that computes an output of n bits, it typically takes only about $2^{n/2}$ trials to find a collision. So, we need to define cryptographic hash functions with sufficient length, n, where $2^{n/2}$ trials is still too large to try by brute force.

For example, the Secure Hash Algorithm, SHA-1, has a 160 bit output. Hence, by the birthday paradox analogy, we would expect that it would take about 2^{80} trials to find a collision. However, recently a collision was found in only 2^{69} trials, which is about 2,000 times faster. Both MD5 and SHA-1 have theoretically been broken, i.e., collisions were found with much fewer than the mathematical expected value of $2^{n/2}$ trials. Hence, NIST recently had a competition for the next Advanced Hash Standard (AHS) to replace SHA [30]. The finalist has been chosen in 2012.

We note that theoretical collisions are not necessarily integrity breaches, since in practice, the collisions have to make sense, i.e., the two messages that have the same hash value must be meaningful messages. However, if the number of possible hash values 2^n is not very large, it may be possible to construct a *birthday attack* (see Section 4.3).

The birthday paradox analogy for collisions illustrates why hash function outputs need to be longer than ciphertext blocks: It takes only $2^{n/2}$ trials to break a hash function (i.e., find a collision), whereas it takes 2^{n-1} trials to break a symmetric-key block cipher.

4.2.3 HASH FUNCTIONS FOR INTEGRITY

Hash functions can be used to detect integrity breaches. Let the sender compute h(M), the hash of message M, then send M, h(M). At the receiving end, the recipient can verify that the message M' received has not been tampered with, by recomputing h(M'). If h(M) = h(M'), then M=M', because of the collision resistance of hash function h().

However, h(M) has to be kept or sent securely. Otherwise, the attacker can just change M to M1, and compute h(M1), and send (M1, h(M1)) instead. Because of this possible attack, keyed-hash functions have been introduced.

4.2.4   KEYED-HASH OR MAC

A *keyed-hash* function, also called a *Message Authentication Code*, MAC, is a hash function that takes as input a secret key K, in addition to the messsage M:

$$MAC(M) = h(M, K).$$

Now, the sender sends M, h(M,K). If the attacker wants to change the message to M1, he will not be able to compute h(M1, K) since he does not have the secret key, K. He would have to send M1, h(M,K). The recipient re-computes the hash of the message M1 sent and compares this with the hash sent. Since h(M1,K) will not equal h(M,K), the recipient finds that he cannot "verify the hash" and hence detects that the message has been tampered with.

It turns out that just appending, or prepending, the key K to the message M before computing the hash function is not secure enough. To maximize the security of a keyed-hash function, two hashes should be computed, as in the *HMAC function*. Defined as RFC 2104:

$$HMAC(M,K) = h(K \oplus opad, h(K \oplus ipad, M)),$$

where ipad = 0x36 and opad = 0x56, each repeated S times, and S is the number of bytes in a message block (i.e., 64 for MD5 and SHA).

The constants, ipad and opad are called "whiteners", to protect the secret key, K.

4.2.5   HASH TREES

When we need to compute and re-compute the hash of a very large amount of data, in order to see if it has been changed, a hash tree is often more efficient. Only $\log_k(n)$ hashes have to be done, fetching only k leaves (data lines). Without a tree of hashes, all n leaves have to be fetched to compute the hash in a linear rather than logarithmic fashion.

A *hash tree* is a tree of hashes. The leaves of the tree are hashes of non-overlapping chunks of the original data whose integrity is to be protected. Each parent node is the hash of its child nodes, and all intermediate nodes of the hash tree are themselves hashes. The *root* of the hash tree is a *root hash* value that will reflect the integrity of the whole data (i.e., the integrity of all the leaves and the intermediate tree nodes). Figure 4.8 shows a hash tree where each parent node has four child nodes.

A hash tree saves having to compute the hash of the whole data when only a small part of the data is changed. Only the hashes on the path from the leaf (that contains the data that is changed) to the root has to be re-computed. Similarly, to verify the integrity of a chunk of the data, only the hashes on the path from the leaf to the root has to be checked and verified.

When a hash tree is used, the amount of storage that has to be secure is also reduced. Without a hash tree, each hash of each leaf node needs to be stored securely. However, with a hash tree, only the root of the hash tree needs to be stored securely. The intermediate hashes can be stored in insecure storage, since their integrity is vouched for by their parent hash, and that eventually is vouched for by the root hash of the hash tree—which the attacker cannot modify since it is in secure storage.

A hash tree is also called an *integrity tree* or a *Merkle tree* [31] (after the name of the person who first proposed hashes organized as a tree).

While a hash tree seems "efficient" to a cryptographer, since it reduces O(n) operations to O(log n) operations, having to do log n memory operations for every memory access sounds prohibitively expensive to most computer architects. Hence, many papers have been written by computer architects on making this faster—the real challenge may be to come up with something better than a hash tree.

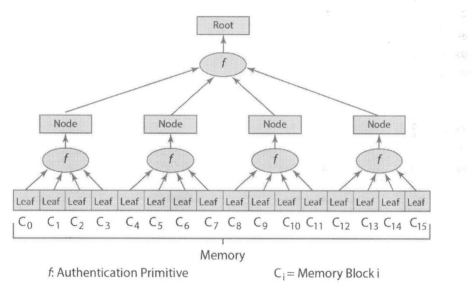

Figure 4.8: A 4-ary hash tree for integrity verification.

For example, to protect the main memory of a computer from physical attacks on it which modify the memory's contents, a *memory integrity tree* is often used. This is just a hash tree over the main memory. Figure 4.8 shows a memory integrity tree over a tiny memory with 16 memory blocks (each memory block mapping into a cache line). There are only two levels of non-leaf nodes in this tree. If there are 4 Gigabytes (2^{32} bytes) of memory, then there will be $\log_4(2^{32})$ = 16 levels of nodes in the memory integrity tree.

Many papers have been written about protecting the integrity of memory from physical attacks with a memory integrity tree (MIT) (see Appendix: Further Readings). Sometimes, systems with a MIT are often erroneously termed "secure processors." This is unfortunate terminology, since a secure processor should provide protection from software attacks as well—not just from physical attacks, and should provide confidentiality—not just integrity. Furthermore, secure processors should consider attacks on computation, storage, etc.—not just attacks on the memory.

4.2.6 USE OF BLOCK CIPHERS AS HASH FUNCTIONS

A block cipher, in CBC mode, can be used as a keyed-hash function. Consider AES_CBC_MAC, which is just the AES algorithm in Cipher Block Chaining mode, used as a Message Authentication Code. Recall that CBC mode used the ciphertext of the previous block and the plaintext of the current block to compute the ciphertext of the current block—thus all plaintext blocks are used in the computation of the final ciphertext block. Hence, if we throw away all the intermediate ciphertext blocks, and just keep the final ciphertext block, this is like a keyed hash of the entire message. The blocksize of AES is 128 bits, which is shorter than most hash functions, but probably long enough for many runtime data/code integrity scenarios.

When the cryptography module is in hardware, using AES_CBC_MAC for the MAC function means that only one AES implementation is needed for both encryption/decryption for confidentiality protection, and again as keyed-hash generation/verification for integrity protection [25]. This is useful in devices with constrained resources, such as mobile devices and sensors.

4.2.7 EXAMPLES OF USE

Hash functions have many uses. They can be used to detect integrity breaches, i.e., unauthorized modification of some information (data, code or file), as shown earlier. This is also called detection of data corruption or tampering, or protection of message integrity.

A hash can also be used as a *fingerprint* of a message, or of a file, or of any object.

A new use of hashes (demonstrated in the Bastion security architecture [36, 37]) is as the *unique identity of a code module*. If we want to make sure that the code module has not been changed by an attacker, e.g., that malware has not been inserted into the code module, we can take a hash of the good code module and use that to identify the code module (like a unique global name). The same code module with malware would have a different identity or hash value. Also, two identical code modules, but with different filenames, would have the same hash value, and hence the same identity.

Hashes are also used to make digital signatures more efficient. Later, we will discuss signing with a private key (from a public-private key-pair). Public-key encryption is a much more computationally expensive operation than symmetric-key encryption. Hence, rather than use private-key signing of a long document, we can first hash the document, then sign the hash using a private-key encryption operation. (We will discuss this in detail later in the Public-key cryptography section.)

Hashes can also be used to provide a form of confidentiality (due to their one-way function property) in addition to change resistance (due to their collision resistance property). For example, consider an online auction where people enter bids, which they do not want others to see. If each enters the hash of his or her bid, others cannot tell what the bid actually is, so the bid can be posted publicly. When the auction ends, no person can change his or her bid from \$x to \$y, since $h(y) \neq h(x)$, due to the collision resistance property. Each bidder can reveal his or her bid, which can be verified by computing the hash of the bid and verifying with the hash value he or she submitted earlier.

4.2.8   COMPUTER ARCHITECTURE EXAMPLES

Hardware trust anchors for confidentiality and integrity

Figure 4.9 shows how two hardware trust anchors, a Device Root Key and a Storage Root Hash, are sufficient to provide confidentiality and integrity protection for secure storage in the authority-mode SP architecture [26]. This secure storage can be built on any untrusted storage using encryption for confidentiality and a hash tree for integrity. By using the secure storage to store keys and security policies, any number of other files and objects can also be cryptographically protected for confidentiality and integrity.

In general, SP first showed that any (non-volatile) storage or (volatile) memory can be cryptographically protected by encryption and hashing, with only two hardware trust anchors: a master key and a root hash. These two hardware registers must be carefully protected by hardware. They are the trust anchors that protect the confidentiality and the integrity of the storage or memory component.

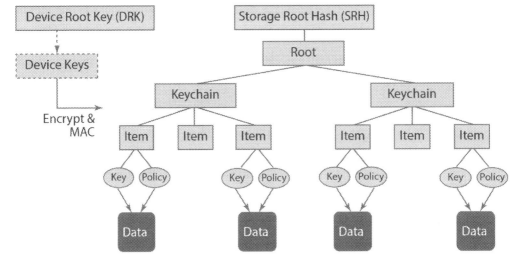

Figure 4.9: Hardware-enabled secure storage.

Many other proposals for secure processors have been made, including [36, 37, 38, 39]. See also the list of Secure Processor papers in the Appendix at the end of the book.

Memory Integrity attacks

Imagine storing a value A to a memory location, but retrieving a different value on subsequent reading from that memory location—with this unauthorized modification of that memory location done by an attacker. It would be impossible to have a rational programming model if what you stored in memory is not what you get back.

There are at least three types of attacks on Memory Integrity:

- A *spoofing attack* is when the value in a memory location is illegitimately changed to another value

- A *splicing attack* is when the contents of two memory locations are exchanged

- A *replay attack* is when a stale memory value is presented instead of its fresh value

A keyed-hash of the contents can protect a cache-line from spoofing attacks only. A keyed-hash that includes the address of the cache-line can also protect against splicing attacks—but cannot protect against replay attacks. A memory integrity tree can protect against spoofing, splicing and replay attacks. In a memory integrity tree, the *root hash* stores the hash over the whole memory that is protected by cryptographic hashes. On reading a last-level cache line into the processor chip from external memory, a hash check operation is performed. On writing a last-level cache line to external memory, a hash update operation is done. On each of these operations, the hash values in the nodes along the path from the leaf node to the root node are checked (on reading) or updated (on writing).

To improve performance, if the nodes of a memory integrity tree are cached on the processor chip, then the checking or updating only has to proceed to the first cached parent node, and not to the root [32]. This is because values inside the processor chip are considered trusted (in most secure processor threat models), whereas all other hardware outside of the microprocessor chip are considered vulnerable to physical attacks, including the main memory.

Hardware proposals for implementing a memory integrity tree to protect the memory (DRAM) of a computer from physical attacks on its integrity are given in Appendix: Further Readings.

An interesting and creative optimization of a memory integrity tree is called a Bonsai tree [24]. A Bonsai tree is a hash tree over the counters, rather than over the entire memory (see Figure 4.10). Hence, it is significantly smaller and faster. The Bonsai tree for protecting memory integrity was coupled with a counter-mode encryption scheme for memory encryption. This counter-mode encryption used logical IDs for pages—rather than either a virtual page number or a physical page number, both of which have their problems.

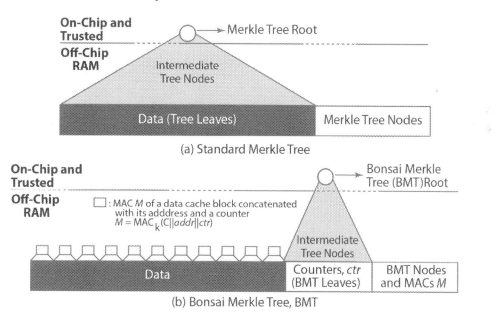

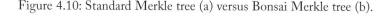

Figure 4.10: Standard Merkle tree (a) versus Bonsai Merkle tree (b).

Various other proposals for memory integrity trees are also surveyed in [33], and cited in the list of Memory Integrity Tree papers at the end of the book.

4.3   MORE ON THE BIRTHDAY PARADOX (OPTIONAL)

To illustrate the weak and strong collision properties, the "birthday paradox" analogy is often helpful.

Analogous to weak collision resistance, we ask "How many people must there be in a room so that the probability is greater than half that someone has a birthday on April 15?" Let's call this a specific collision. By first finding the probability that people do NOT have a birthday on April 15, and assuming 365 days in a year, we can subtract this probability from 1 and solve for N in the equation:

$$\tfrac{1}{2} = 1 - (364/365)^N,$$

which gives the answer, N = 253 people.

Analogous to strong collision resistance, we ask "How many people must there be in a room so that the probability is greater than half that two people have the same birthday?" Let's call this random collision. By solving for N in the equation:

$$\tfrac{1}{2} = 1 - 365*364*\ldots *(365-N+1)/365^N,$$

we get the answer N=23 people.

To have N people where none have the same birthday, the first person can have a birthday on any of 365 days, the next on any of 364 days,..., and the Nth person on any of 365-N+1 days. (Without the restriction of duplicates, all N people can have their birthday on any of 365 days.) Hence, the probability that none of N people have a birthday on the same day is $365*364*\ldots(365-N+1)/365^N$. Subtracting from 1, we get the probability that at least two people have the same birthday.

While this may at first seem a surprisingly small number, it is not that surprising if one realizes that it should be around sqrt(365), which is around 19, since we are comparing all *pairs* of people to see if they have the same birthday.

Hence, for a hash function that computes an output of n bits, it takes about 2^n trials to find a specific collision, but only $2^{n/2}$ trials to find a random collision. So, we need to define cryptographic hash functions where $2^{n/2}$ trials is still too large to try by brute force.

We note that theoretical collisions are not necessarily integrity breaches, since in practice, the collisions have to make sense, i.e., the two messages that have the same hash value must be meaningful messages. However, if the number of possible hash values 2^n is not very large, it may be possible to construct a *birthday attack* as follows:

1. Generate $2^{n/2}$ versions of the original message, x. Generate the hash values H(x) for each of these.

2. Generate $2^{n/2}$ versions of the fraudulant message, y. Generate the hash H(y) for each of these.

3. Find a hash value H(x)= H(y). If none exist, keep generating more of 1 and 2 until find a matching pair of hash values.

4. Get the signature of Alice, with her private key, on the version of the original message with the matching hash value.

5. Later, can send the fraudulent message with this digital signature.

It is not too difficult to generate many versions of a message. For example, use extra spaces between words, use synonyms, and reorder phrases and sentences, where this does not change the meaning.

CHAPTER 5

Public-Key Cryptography

Public-key cryptography is used for establishing longer-term identities in cyberspace. It is used for authentication of users, programs, devices or systems. It can provide non-repudiation, and is used in digital signatures. Non-repudiation and digital signatures will be defined in later sections.

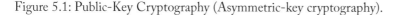

Figure 5.1: Public-Key Cryptography (Asymmetric-key cryptography).

Unlike symmetric-key cryptography, where the same secret key is used for encryption by the sender and decryption by the recipient, public-key cryptography uses two keys: one for encryption and another for decryption. This is called a *key-pair*: the two keys are not arbitrary keys, but a matched pair of keys. Public-key crypto is also called asymmetric-key crypto (see Figure 5.1).

A motivation for public-key crypto is the difficulty of sending the secret key for symmetric-key ciphers to the recipient, over public networks. In public-key crypto, the encryption key for Bob is known publicly, and is called the public key; but the decryption key is private and only known by Bob. Anyone can use Bob's public key to encrypt a message for Bob; only Bob having his private key can correctly decrypt this message. I call this *targeted encryption*.

The private key can also be used for encryption. In this case, when Alice uses her private key to encrypt a message, it is as if she *signed* the message, since she is the only one who has access to her private key. Anyone can use Alice's public key to decrypt this message and thus *verify* that it is indeed Alice who signed it.

Hence, the private key of someone's key-pair is like their digital *identity*. An operation done with Alice's private key can authenticate the person as Alice. A request signed by Alice's private key provides *non-repudiation*: Alice cannot deny that she made that request, since she is supposed to be the only person that has that private key. We discuss digital signatures and non-repudiation in more detail below.

The importance of keeping one's private key confidential cannot be over-emphasized, since this is the crux of one's longer-term digital identity. If one's private key is lost or somehow accessible by an attacker, all the security provided by public-key cryptography becomes null and void.

It should be clear that a private key can also be used to identify a piece of software, a chip, a hardware device, a computer or a system, in addition to identifying a person.

5.1   DIGITAL SIGNATURE

A digital signature is used to bind the signer to an original (i.e., un-modified) version of a document, X. To ensure the integrity of the document that was signed, a hash function H(X) is computed over the document. This hash function is then signed (i.e., encrypted) with the private key of the signer, $[H(X)]_{SK}$. The hash function thus also serves as a performance enhancer, since the private key encryption need only be done over a small hash value, rather than over a long document. The document and its signature are then sent out to recipients, as shown in Figure 5.2.

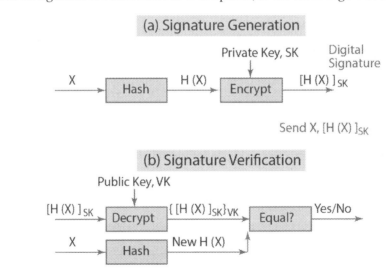

Figure 5.2: Digital signature (a) generation and (b) verification.

Figure 5.2 shows a common notation for private key operations, using square brackets [ ] subscripted with the private key used. A public-key operation is denoted with curly brackets { }, subscripted with the public key used.

The recipient can verify that the document is unchanged and that it was signed by the owner of the private key SK. The public-key VK is used to decrypt the signature. At the same time, a new hash of the document X can be computed. This is then compared with the decrypted value of the signature. If the old and new hash values are the same, then the document is unchanged, and the digital signature is verified. Otherwise, the digital signature verification fails.

We sometimes abbreviate the digital signature X, $[H(X)]_{SK}$ as just $\text{Sig}(X)_{Alice}$, the digital signature of Alice on X.

5.2   NON-REPUDIATION

As long as the private key is carefully guarded by its owner and not accessible to anyone but its owner, the owner cannot deny (i.e., repudiate) that she or he performed any operation that uses the private key. Hence, digital signatures have the non-repudiation property.

Non-repudiation is not true for symmetric-key operations. If Alice sends Bob a message encrypted by the symmetric key she shares with Bob, she can later deny that she sent that message, since she can insist that Bob could have created that message himself, since he has the same symmetric key.

5.3   PUBLIC-PRIVATE KEY-PAIRS

Best security practices dictate that you do not use the same private key for your digital signature as you would for decrypting messages sent to you. This means that each user should ideally have at least two public-private key-pairs, as shown in Figure 5.3. Alice has a private decryption key DK_A with its correpponding public encryption key EK_A available to everyone, possibly stored in a public repository. She has another key-pair, (SK_A, VK_A), where she guards her private key SK_A "with her life"—as it is her digital identity—and uses it for generating her digital signature. The correesponding public key, VK_A, is available publicly to everyone, and can be used to verify Alice's digital signature. Similarly, Bob has two key-pairs associated with him for targeted encryption to him, and for him to sign messages, data or programs.

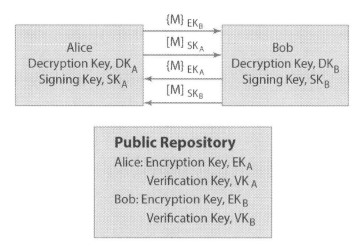

Figure 5.3: Associating two key-pairs with each user.

We use curly brackets $\{M\}_K$ to indicate a public-key operation on message M using the public-key K. We use square brackets $[M]_K$ to indicate a private key operation on M using the private key K. (To help remember this notation, think of the square brackets as being the more restrictive operation, performed only by one person, whereas curly brackets are more inclusive and can be performed by many people.)

If Alice wants to send Bob a message M that only Bob can decrypt, she encrypts it with Bob's public key and sends $\{M\}_{EK_B}$. This can be written equivalently as $\{M\}_{Bob}$ for clarity. Note that anyone, including an attacker, can encrypt a message for Bob using his public key, and Bob cannot be sure who the sender is. But since Bob is the only one that can decrypt the message with his private key to get back the plaintext $M = [\{M\}_{EK_B}]_{DK_B}$, confidentiality of the message is preserved.

When Alice wants to sign a message so that Bob will know it came from her, she can use her private signing key to encrypt M, generating $[M]_{SK_A}$, which we can also denote equivalently as $[M]_{Alice}$. Note that not just Bob, but anyone can verify Alice's signature by "decrypting" with Alice's public verification key, $\{[M]_{SK_A}\}_{VK_A} = M$. Hence, confidentiality is not preserved, but non-repudiation by Alice is preserved.

Note that the sender of the message signed by Alice need not be Alice, and in fact can be an adversary, forwarding this message signed by Alice. However, as long as only Alice has access to her private signing key, no one else can generate her private key operation, $[M]_{SK_A}$, and non-repudiation by Alice, the signer of the message, is achieved.

Hence, to achieve both confidentiality of the message M and non-repudiation, it may be desirable to do both a targeted encryption for Bob and sign it by Alice. However, it turns out that even doing these two encryptions may not be sufficient due to Man-in-the-Middle attacks on public-key cryptography. It is very important to understand that Man-in-the-Middle attacks are possible in public-key cryptography, since anyone—including an attacker—can do a public-key operation with someone's public key. There are many subtle consequences of encrypting then signing, versus signing then encrypting (see Section 5.10). Depending on the scenario, one could be better than the other. Problems arise because the recipient, the sender or someone else can play the role of the Man-in-the-Middle attacker, using public keys [7].

5.4 PUBLIC-KEY CIPHERS

5.4.1 RSA

There are many public-key algorithms [41, 42]. One of the most well known is RSA, where the cipher's name was derived from the first letters of their inventors: Rivest, Shamir and Adelman. They received the Turing award for this work.

RSA uses modular exponentiation of large numbers for both encryption and decryption, as shown in Figure 5.4. Encryption involves using a public key composed of an exponent and a modulus, (e, N). The plaintext M is raised to the power of e, taken modulo N. Decryption takes the ciphertext C raised to the power of d, which is the private key, modulo N. The key-pair is (e, N) and d, where e and d are related as follows:

$$ed \equiv 1 \ (mod \ (p\text{-}1)(q\text{-}1)), \ where \ N = pq,$$

p and q are large primes, with e relatively prime to (p-1)(q-1).

The trap-door, one-way function used in RSA is integer factorization, which is known as a hard mathematical problem.

To generate a new key-pair, first find two large primes (typically on the order of 1,024 or 2,048 bits each), and multiply them together to give the modulus N. Then find a number e which is relatively prime to (p-1)(q-1). Then find the inverse of e mod ((p-1)(q-1)), which will be the private key d.

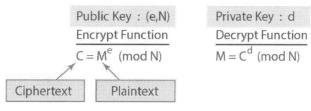

Figure 5.4: RSA public-key cipher.

Although the RSA encryption and decryption functions look deceptively simple, public-key cryptography is about three orders of magnitude slower than symmetric-key cryptography, when both are done in software. The exponentiation of a thousand-bit number with an exponent that is also about a thousand bits long, is very computationally intensive. Fortunately, such public-key operations need not be used as often as symmetric-key crypto. In section 5.7, we show how public-key crypto can be used to send a symmetric key, which can then be used more efficiently for bulk encryption.

5.4.2   OTHER PUBLIC-KEY CRYPTOGRAPHY ALGORITHMS

There are many other public-key crypto algorithms. They are all based on some difficult mathematical function where going one way is computationally feasible, but the inverse is computationally infeasible.

For example, the Diffie-Hellman (DH) key-exchange algorithm can be used to generate a shared secret key between two or more parties over a public network. (However, a Man-in-the-Middle attack exists.)

Another class of public-key ciphers are called Elliptic Curve Cryptography (ECC). This is based on elliptic curves, and can use much shorter public and private keys than RSA, for an equivalent level of security.[5]

The interested reader can read up on more cryptography algorithms in [42], learn the mathematics behind the ciphers by reading [41] and read any of a plethora of books on cryptography.

5.5   USES OF PUBLIC-KEY CRYPTOGRAPHY

We now summarize some of the main uses of public-key algorithms. Public-key cryptography is used primarily for establishing long-term digital identities. As such, it is useful for the authentication of a person or device.

It is also used for digital signatures, which provides integrity and non-repudiation for the messages, documents, or information that are hashed and signed.

It can be used to achieve confidentiality, providing targeted encryption, using the public key of a recipient who holds the matching private key. This can be used to transmit critical sensitive information, like secret symmetric keys, over an insecure channel or public network, for subsequent use in bulk encryption. The Diffie Hellman algorithm can be used for key-exchange.

The main pitfall of public-key protocols is that they have Man-in-the-Middle attacks. A Man-in-the-Middle attack is when an adversary intercepts all messages between a sender and a recipient, and has the ability to eavesdrop, change, drop or insert messages. Recall that in public-key crypto, anyone (including an adversary "in the middle") can do a public-key operation, even though only the owner of the private key can do a private-key operation. If this fact is not clearly understood, then the recipient can misinterpret the message he receives, since it could come from a Man-in-the-Middle attacker (doing a public-key operation) rather than the legitimate sender. The interested reader can peruse Section 5.10 for examples of such attacks. We also discuss Man-in-the-Middle attacks further in Chapter 6 on security protocols.

5.6   PUBLIC-KEY INFRASTRUCTURE (PKI)

For public-key cryptography to work in practice, a public-key infrastructure has to be set up. This includes public-key certificates, trusted third parties to issue these certificates, and many other issues. We discuss some of them below.

5.6.1   PUBLIC-KEY CERTIFICATES AND CERTIFICATE AUTHORITIES

Let's examine Figure 5.3 again. The public repository holds the public keys for Alice, Bob and anyone who wants to post a public key. But what if an attacker Eve pretended to be Alice and posted

---

[5]   In the future, there may also be stronger interest in ECC because of Shor's algorithm for factoring the product of two primes on a quantum computer.

public keys for Alice that are actually paired with private keys that Eve has? How can we be sure that those are really the public keys belonging to Alice?

For this, we can have some Trusted Third Parties (TTPs) called Certificate Authorities (CAs) who will vouch that the public keys actually belong to a given person, in a certificate. A Certificate Authority is like the Department of Motor Vehicles (DMV); it will use some other means to check that Alice White is indeed Alice White before issuing a driver's license or identity card to her. A CA is the trusted entity that issues public-key certificates. In the case of public keys, a public-key certificate certifies that the enclosed public keys indeed belong to Alice White, and this certification is achieved by signing with the private key of the CA. Figure 5.5 shows the contents of a certificate. While the main purpose of a certificate is to associate the user's name with his or her public keys, other information may also be included like the time period for which the certiciate is valid. The most important part is the digital signature of the CA, which vouches for the contents of the certificate.

$$\mathbf{Cert_A = C_A \,||\, [h(C_A)]_{SKs}}$$

where $C_A = (T_s, L, A, EK_A, VK_A)$,

$[h(x)]_y$ is the digital signature of x with private key y, and

T_s is the certificate start date,
L is the length of time this certificate is valid,
A is the certificate owner's name,
EK_A is the owner's public encryption key,
VK_A is the owner's public signature verification key,
h(x) is the cryptographic hash of x,
SKs is the private signing key of Certificate Authority S.

Figure 5.5: Public-key certificate for A signed by certificate authority S.

Certificates need not be retrieved by a recipient from a public-key certificate repository, although this is also possible. A certificate can be sent by a sender when he sends his public key to the recipient. The recipient must have the public key of the CA that signed the certificate, and must trust this CA—otherwise, he or she need not trust the certificate.

5.6.2 TYPES OF PUBLIC-KEY INFRASTRUCTURES

The use of certificates and CAs increase the trustworthiness of public keys. However, CAs must be set up, which takes time. In general, it is not practical to have just one CA for all possible users worldwide. Typical, there is a hierarchy of CAs. A local CA signs the certificates for users in its organization. Another CA then signs the certificates of these local CAs, and so forth (see Figure 5.6). For example, certificates for Princeton faculty, staff and students may be signed by the local Princeton CA, the certificate for the Princeton CA may be signed by a NJ-state CA, etc. This results in Alice sending her public key, with a bunch of certificates, each signed by the "higher" CA in this CA hierarchy. (In practice, such a complete chain of CAs is not set up, and only the local CA signs a user's certificate. Also, a single root CA is not likely to be trusted by all countries, nor even within a country, and so mutiple "root CAs" are present.)

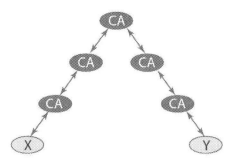

Figure 5.6: Hierarchy of Certificate Authorities.

Instead of a CA hierarchy, the PKI trust model can also consist of multiple CAs, with the user deciding which CA to trust. For example, a web browser may have over 80 certificates to verify signatures.

For public-key cryptography to work, a Public Key Infrastructure (PKI) must first be established. A PKI consists of all the pieces needed to make public-key cryptography work. First, it needs to set up trusted entities as Certificate Authorities and establish their hierarchical trust structure, if any. There must be agreed upon requirements for a CA and what it must do to verify that a person wanting a certicate is genuinely that person. CAs should be periodically reviewed in order to remain trusted CAs.

Second, there must be standard formats for certificates. For example, X.509 is a standard for public-key certificates.

Third, there must be agreed upon ways to generate new public-private key-pairs that are cryptographically secure.

Fourth, there must be a standard way to revoke certificates, when a private key corresponding to a public key in a certificate is stolen (i.e., compromised) before the expiration time of the certificate. This can be done in a similar way to credit card revocations for stolen credit cards: a Certificate Revocation List (CRL) must be set up, and users should check this CRL before trusting the certificate. This CRL should be updated daily (or more frequently for high security facilities). The problem is there is still a window of vulnerability between the time the private key is compromised and the time the CRL is updated; furthermore, many users and their systems just do not check CRLs.

5.6.3   WEB OF TRUST

Can public-key crypto be used without setting up a PKI? This can be done if each user essentially serves as a CA for the people he trusts. He vouches for these people and their public keys by signing "certificates" for them. For example, Alice does not know David, but Alice knows Bob who vouches for Charlie, who vouches for David. There is a chain of certificates by which Alice could get David's public encryption and signature verification keys:

$$\text{Sig[Bob, EK}_B\text{, VK}_B]_{\text{Alice}}, \quad \text{Sig[Charlie, EK}_C\text{, VK}_C]_{\text{Bob}}, \quad \text{Sig[David, EK}_D\text{, VK}_D]_{\text{Charlie}}$$

It is up to Alice to decide if she trusts this chain, and hence whether she trusts the public keys of David derived through this chain. This is called a *web of trust*. It is used in PGP, which stands for Pretty Good Privacy.

5.7   EFFICIENT USE OF PUBLIC-KEY AND SYMMETRIC-KEY CRYPTO

Public-key cryptography is used to establish key pairs for longer-term identities in cyberspace. It is then used to establish session keys and/or symmetric keys, which are then used for *bulk encryption*, i.e., the encryption of large amounts of data. Although public-key ciphers can perform encryption for confidentiality, they are rarely used for bulk encryption because public-key encryption and decryption can take three orders of magnitude longer than symmetric-key encryption and decryption.

Also, it is much more expensive generating a public-private key-pair compared to generating a new symmetric-key. Hence, frequently public-key cryptography is used to set up a key-pair for longer-term identity, then used just to establish a shared symmetric key with the other party for bulk encryption.

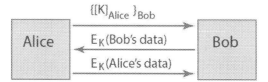

Figure 5.7: Confidentiality using both public-key and symmetric-key crypto.

Figure 5.7 shows Alice sending a new symmetric key, K, to Bob, signed by her private signing key and then encrypted with Bob's public encryption key. This assumes that Alice and Bob have each set up at least one key-pair each, and that they have authenticated each other and verified the other's public key via certificates or some other method.

5.8   EXAMPLE: SECURE SOCKETS LAYER

Next, we look at a real-world protocol for establishing a secure communications channel, within an untrusted (insecure) public network, that can protect the confidentiality and integrity of communications between two parties, Alice and Bob. The SSL protocol (Secure Sockets Layer) is one of the most widely used Internet protocols. It is also called TLS (Transport Layer Protocol) and is used in the secure version of the http protocol, called https where the "s" stands for "secure" (and "http" stands for "hyper text transfer protocol").

SSL consists of two parts: SSL handshake and SSL Record, as shown in Figure 5.8. The SSL handshake uses a public-key certificate to authenticate the server to Alice (and optionally uses public-key crypto to authenticate Alice by verifying her digital signature), and establishes a shared secret symmetric key with her if authentication passes. This shared secret symmetric key is also called a *session key*.

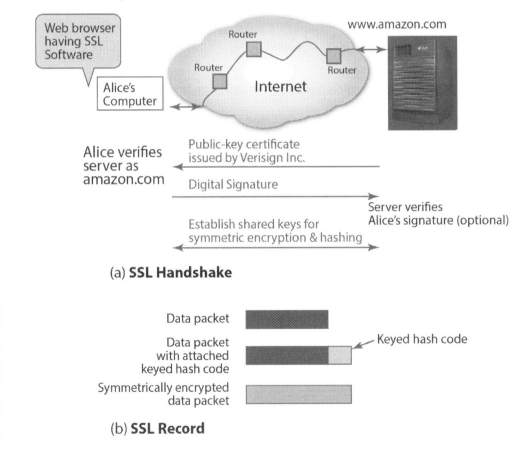

Figure 5.8: SSL Protocol: SSL Handshake (a) and SSL Record (b).

The SSL handshake uses this session key to generate two other symmetric keys—one to be used to generate a keyed-hash of each data packet for protection against integrity breaches, and another for encryption of the data packet (including the keyed-hash) for protection against confidentiality breaches. More detailed discussion of this SSL protocol is given in Section 6.4.

5.9   COMPUTER ARCHITECTURE EXAMPLE: BASTION

We now give an example of how the three types of cryptography we have discussed can be incorporated effectively into a computer architecture.

Bastion [36, 37] is an example of a secure processor architecture that provides fine-grained integrity and confidentiality protection. It provides a "general-purpose" security solution by using software to implement convenient and flexible software security mechanisms, then using hardware to protect these software security mechanisms. In this section, we will describe only the cryptography-related aspects of the Bastion architecture. They include the use of:

- hashes for *module identities* for trusted software modules

- cryptographically protected *secure storage* areas for the hypervisor and for different trusted software modules from mutually suspicious trusted domains; these are cryptographically protected for confidentiality and integrity with only two hardware trust anchors (new hardware registers)

- cryptographically protected *secure memory* using two renewable trust anchors (memory encryption key, memory root hash) that change every session for providing memory integrity and confidentiality

- an enhanced memory integrity tree for detecting physical integrity attacks on the memory as well as confidentiality breaches

- public-key cryptography, certificates and protocols for trust evidence attestation [37]

We will use a microprocessor enhanced with Bastion security features to show how the three basic types of cryptography algorithms we have described (symmetric-key encryption, cryptographic hashes and public-key cryptography) can be applied in secure processor design.

Bastion's goal is to protect security-critical software modules within an untrusted software stack. The architecture provides resilient execution of security-critical tasks even in the presence of (unrelated) corrupted code and malware in the software stack. It must support scalability to multiple mutually suspicious trust domains, not just one trusted domain and one untrusted one. It must provide a mechanism for reporting trust evidence.

Its threat model assumes that attackers can attain root privileges, i.e., even the powerful Operating System (O.S.) can be an adversary. It considers physical attacks in addition to software attacks in its threat model. Its trusted computing base (TCB) includes only the microprocessor chip and the hypervisor. The rest of the hardware and software need not be trusted.

Its hardware-software security mechanisms include the hardware protecting the hyperviser, and the hyperviser protecting the other trusted software modules. Also, for the hardware, only the processor needs to be trusted, and cryptographic techniques are used to maintain security in the untrusted hardware components, like memory, storage and buses.

Figure 5.9 shows a block diagram of the Bastion architecture in a typical virtual machine environment. It shows a computer with a hypervisor managing the hardware resources for two Virtual Machines: one running a Windows O.S. and the other running the Linux O.S. Bastion leverages this virtualized environment, since it is very common in both client computers and Cloud Computing servers today.

Rather than expect the entire hardware platform to be trusted, Bastion only requires that the microprocessor chip be trusted. In particular, the main memory is not trusted (unlike the assumptions for the industry consortium's Trusted Platform Module (TPM) chip [40] where the entire hardware box is trusted, including the main memory and buses). Similarly, rather than requiring the entire software stack to be trusted, Bastion only requires the hypervisor to be trusted. In particular, the guest OS in the VM is not required to be trusted to run the trusted software modules A, B and C (shown in grey) within untrusted applications on an untrusted commodity OS.

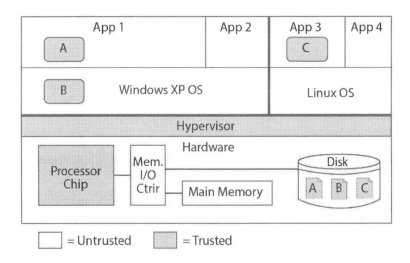

Figure 5.9: Bastion hardware-software security architecture.

For example, module A could be a security monitor running inside the virtual address space of Application 1, which it may be monitoring for security breaches. Clearly, it is important to protect module A from an attacker who might exploit some security vulnerability in App1 or some other Application, to infiltrate the system and attack module A. Bastion also protects module A from a malicious or compromised OS.[6]

Figure 5.9 also shows module B, which is a trusted software module in the OS. Bastion supports trusted software modules in either application space or OS space. Module C is another trusted software module in a different Virtual Machine. These different modules illustrate that Bastion is scalable with respect to both the number of trusted software modules and the number of mutually suspicious trust domains which it can support simultaneously with the same small set of hardware processor extensions, the key aspects of which we describe below.

Module Identities. Bastion introduces the use of a cryptographic hash to represent a trusted module's identity in a secure processor. By the collision resistance property of cryptographic hashes, no two different modules will have the same hash—hence this is a "unique global identifier" for the module. Furthermore, if the module has been injected with malware or has somehow been changed in an unauthorized fashion, its cryptographic hash will not be the same as that of a correct module. Also, while two pieces of code may have different procedure names, if they are identical, they will have the same hash value. Untrusted modules share the module identity of "zero".

Bastion has a **current module id register** that is compared with the module identity added to TLB entries and to the secure storage table in Figure 5.10 (described below), so that the Bastion hypervisor and hardware enforces secure storage accesses bound to each trusted module.

Secure Storage. Bastion architecture provides each trusted module (A, B or C) with its own **secure storage** (shown as grey components labeled A, B, or C, in the disk). This is not a fixed contiguous portion of the disk or online storage, but rather any portions of the storage system, which are cryptographically secured: encrypted for confidentiality and hashed for integrity. The hypervisor is also provided its own secure storage area.

The hypervisor's secure storage is secured by hardware registers: the **storage key register** and the **storage hash register** in Figure 5.10. Then, the "soft registers" providing the *secure storage (SS) key and hash* of each module are stored securely in the hypervisor's secure storage. The Bastion hypervisor and hardware ensure that only the correct trusted software module has access to its *SS key* to decrypt its secure storage, and its SS hash to verify the integrity of its secure storage. This secure storage is persistent (a non-volatile memory resource) in that it survives power on-off cycles.

---

[6] In general, an application writer may be very motivated to write a secure application (or secure modules) to protect his security-critical code and data, but he has no control over the commodity OS. While OS vendors are highly motivated to secure their OS, it is such a large and complex piece of code that this is an extremely difficult task. Weekly security updates are evidence of the continuing vulnerability of an OS to attacks, despite the best efforts of OS providers. Bastion thus does not require the OS to be bug-free, but instead protects trusted software modules (e.g., A, B and C) from a malicious or compromised OS.

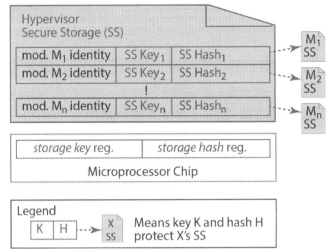

Figure 5.10: Secure Storage (SS) bound to different trusted software modules and to the trusted Hypervisor.

Secure memory. Secure and authenticated memory is also provided to each trusted software module during its execution. This is volatile memory that does not survive power on-off cycles, but must be protected in order to provide a trusted software module with a secure execution environment.

Since the processor chip is the hardware security perimeter for Bastion (as for other secure processors like [25, 26, 38, 39]), confidential data is only available in plaintext in the on-chip caches and registers. Whenever a cache line containing confidential data or code is evicted to off-chip memory, it is first automatically encrypted and hashed with keys that are only accessible by the hardware. These keys are derived from a memory session key for each power-on cycle. This is a key renewal mechanism for further protection of the runtime memory from replay and crypt-analysis attacks.

For memory integrity protection, an enhanced Merkle tree is used. Only the root of this memory integrity tree needs to be kept securely on-chip, in the **memory root hash** register. The leaves of the Merkle tree are in cache line granularity. Bastion also allows only parts of the machine memory to be protected, e.g., those memory pages assigned to the hypervisor and to trusted software modules. This is enabled at the granularity of memory pages.

The **memory session key** and the **memory root hash** are the two hardware trust anchors for runtime memory for all the trusted software and data. Note that these are different from the trust anchors for secure storage. Runtime memory contents are transient (volatile), while storage contents are permanent (non-volatile).

This and other non-cryptographic hardware mechanisms [36, 37] provide a fine-grained, dynamically instantiated, secure execution compartment for trusted software. Hence, Bastion can be used to enable tailored trustworthy spaces within a sea of untrusted software, with hardware-hypervisor architectural support.

Trust evidence attestation. Bastion also provides *trustworthy tailored attestation* [37], which enables a remote party to query the state of the trusted components it requires to perform a security-critical task. This provides a report of the integrity measurements of the trusted software modules required for the security-critical task, and of the hypervisor (see Figure 5.11). This attestation report is unforgeable since it is signed by the chip's private key accessible only to the Bastion hardware. Each Bastion processor chip is issued a unique public-private key-pair, by the hardware vendor or some trusted third party, with the private key securely installed in each chip before deployment in the field. In a typical scenario, the hardware vendor serves as the Certificate Authority, signing the certificate vouching for the public key of the processor chip. The processor can then use its private key to sign the attestation reports generated, when requested, during runtime.

Alice –> Bastion_i: generate attestation (TSM1, TSM2, nonce);

Bastion_i –> Alice: attestation_report containing:

[hash(nonce, hash(hypervisor), hash(TSM1), hash(TSM2))]$_{BiSK}$,

[Bastion_i,BiVK]$_{HWvenSK}$

Figure 5.11: Bastion attestation of trusted components.

In Figure 5.11, (BiSK, BiVK) is the private signing key and public verification key for the Bastion_i processor (Bi), i.e., Bi's key-pair for signing and for verification of this signature. Similarly, (HWvenSK, HWvenVK) is the key-pair for signing and signature verification for the hardware vendor of the Bastion_i processor chip. Square brackets [x]$_K$ indicate the private-key encryption of x using private-key K. Curly brackets {x}$_K$ indicate a public-key operation using public-key K.

Input parameters, configurations and output results of a secure computation can also be included in the attestation report. Attestations can be requested any time, and are very fast.

Other Bastion features. There are, of course, other non-cryptographic features of the Bastion hardware-software architecture that are essential for the security it provides. The interested reader can find these in [36, 37].

5.10 MISUNDERSTANDING PUBLIC-KEY CRYPTO

Many misunderstandings of public-key crypto arise if the recipient does not understand that anyone can perform a public-key operation, and also anyone can act as a Man-in-the-Middle (MiM) and pass along a message encrypted with someone's private key. We illustrate this with two examples below showing the pitfalls of both "sign then encrypt" and "encrypt then sign". Mark Stamp [7] gives an excellent discussion of this.

Sign then Encrypt. Consider trying to achieve both confidentiality and non-repudiation of a message M from Alice to Bob by having Alice sign first with her private key, then encrypt with Bob's public encryption key. Alice can then send this to Bob in the first protocol exchange below. Suppose the message M is "I love you!" Bob can decrypt with his private key and verify Alice's signature with her public key, and see this plaintext message, M.

$$\text{Alice} \to \text{Bob: } \{[M]_{SKA}\}_{EKB}$$

$$;\text{Alice signs M then encrypts this} \tag{1}$$

$$\text{Bob} \to \text{Charlie: } \{[M]_{SKA}\}_{EKC}$$

$$; \text{Bob plays a trick on Charlie} \tag{2}$$

Suppose Bob wants to play a trick on Charlie, he can decrypt with his private key, then re-encrypt Alice's signed message with Charlie's public key, EKC, and send it on to Charlie (second protocol exchange (2)). Charlie may think that Alice sent him a signed message "I love you!"—if he misunderstands public-key cryptography. In this MiM attack, Bob—the rightful recipient of Alice's message, is acting as the Man-in-the-Middle attacker between Alice and Charlie.

In this case, it would have been better to "encrypt then sign":

$$\text{Alice} \to \text{Bob: } [\{M\}_{EKB}]_{SKA}$$

$$;\text{Alice encrypts M for Bob then signs} \tag{3}$$

Bob can verify Alice's signature, then know that he is the only one who could have decrypted the message M with his private decryption key. While he can encrypt M for Charlie with Charlie's public key, he cannot generate Alice's signature over this since he does not have Alice's private signing key.

Encrypt then Sign. In a different scenario, "encrypt then sign" can also be subject to a Man-in the-Middle attack and thus misinterpreted. Suppose that Alice wants to send the publisher, Bob, the results of some important scientific research, where many teams are competing to be the first to publish new results. This is like the protocol exchange (3) except that the message M is "I have the first drug to cure AIDS."

Suppose Charlie is a competitor of Alice, and intercepts the message from Alice to Bob. Since anyone can do a public-key operation, Charlie can peel off Alice's outer encryption, i.e., her signature (by decrypting with Alice's public verification key). While he cannot decrypt the inner encryption since he does not have Bob's private key, he can sign this inner encryption with his own private key, as in (4):

Charlie -> Bob: $[\{M\}_{EKB}]_{SKC}$

;Charlie pretends Alice's messsage is from him (4)

Bob may misunderstand public-key crypto and think that Charlie sent him the message, "I have the first drug to cure AIDS", when actually Alice is the rightful sender. Here, Charlie is the MiM attacker.

Importance of Context. The above examples illustrate that one has to be very careful in designing public-key cryptography protocols, to prevent misinterpretation—there are many subtle pitfalls in misunderstanding the public-key operations. Remember that:

- Anyone can do a public-key operation.

- The sender may not be the signer of the message.

- Public-key protocols must be designed carefully to avoid Man-in-the-Middle (MiM) attacks.

A very simple solution to the above two scenarios is for Alice to include enough information in the message M so that such MiM attacks would fail. For example, in the first scenario, the message can be "Bob, I love you. From Alice." Charlie would then know that the message was not for him when he receives the message in (2).

Similarly, in the second case, if Alice sent the message: "Dear Bob, I am Alice and I have the first drug to cure AIDS." Bob would be able to detect that the message was not likely from Charlie, even though he received a message signed by Charlie.

This leads us into Chapter 6, Security Protocols, where we will look at protocols in more detail.

CHAPTER 6

Security Protocols

Security Protocols are perhaps the most essential and subtle aspects of security architectures. They describe the interactions between different players (or principals) in a distributed computing environment. They can also be used to describe the interactions between components within a single computer.

6.1 PROTOCOL NOTATION

Protocol notation is a convenient linear representation of an interaction between a sender and one or more recipients. It is typically written as:

> Sender -> Recipient: message   ; comments

In network protocols, only what is sent out on the network is placed in the "message" part of the protocol notation. Computations done at either sender or recipient end are indicated within the comments part of the protocol notation.

Some people feel it is clearer to represent protocols in pictorial form, also called protocol diagrams, as shown in Figure 6.1 (a). However, once one is used to reading the linearized protocol notation (Figure 6.1 (b)), it is more compact and often more accurate.

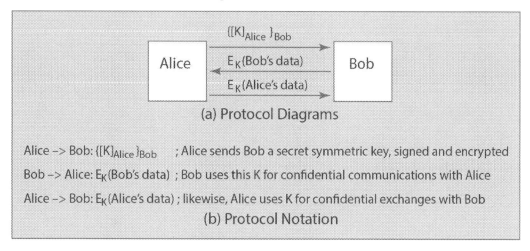

Figure 6.1: Protocol Diagram (a) and Protocol Notation (b).

6.2 CHALLENGE-RESPONSE PROTOCOLS

A Challenge-Response protocol can be used to authenticate someone. For example, an authentication server can send a random number, R, as a challenge to a remote user. The remote user must return a response, which is a function of the random number R and something that only the remote user has that the server can verify, e.g., a password-response generator or the use of his/her private signing key. The authentication server can then check that the response is correct.

Figure 6.2 shows two forms of challenge-response protocols. In Figure 6.2(a), the user, Alice or A, is given a password_generation fob (or gadget) that requires a PIN to enable; it will then calculate a function F on an input R. The user then sends this response back to the authentication server, B. The server can also calculate F(R) and hence verify that the response is correct. This is sometimes called a 2-factor authentication, since the use of the password_generator is "something you have" while the PIN to activate it is "something you know".

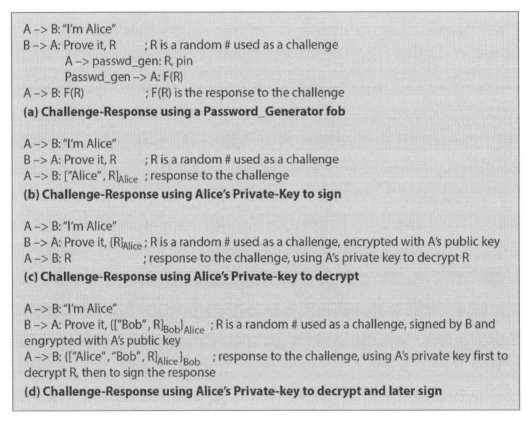

Figure 6.2: Challenge-Response Protocols.

In Figure 6.2(b), public-key cryptography is used instead of a password_generator fob. When issued the random challenge R, Alice returns the encryption of her name "Alice" concatenated with R, encrypted (signed) with her private key. The server B can use Alice's public key to verify the contents. The name "Alice" is inserted into the signature to provide context. The random number R prevents replay attacks, since it is different each time and its value is unpredictable.

The problem with the protocol in Figure 6.2(b) is that an attacker, Eve, intercepting the communication from Alice to Bob, could get Alice to sign anything (which is sent in place of the random challenge R).

Similarly, in Figure 6.2(c), Eve the attacker could get Alice to decrypt anything, if she could intercept the first message from Alice to Bob.

What is needed is for Alice to know that the challenge indeed came from Bob, and not some attacker Eve. Hence, Figure 6.2(d) may be an appropriate solution, which also does not allow Eve to misuse the protocol to get Alice to sign or decrypt something Eve wants. Some context is also added to prevent misunderstanding of the public-key operations.

6.3   PROTOCOL ATTACKS

In a *Replay attack* the attacker captures protocol exchanges over the public network, and later replays this "stale" information to breach integrity or authentication. A Replay attack is composed of two parts: Prior to the attack, the attacker does passive eavesdropping. This is followed by the actual replay attack, where data previously captured by the attacker is used to cause a security breach. This can be an attack on integrity (e.g., replaying a hash value), or a masquerading attack (e.g., replaying a password or digital signature). In a replay attack, the attacker may not be able to decrypt the data, nor generate a new hash or signature, but he may still be able to use the stale data with a good hash or signature, even when this data has been updated—without being detected.

To defeat Replay attacks, "freshness" must be introduced into the protocol. Sometimes a nonce (number used once) is sufficient; other times, not only the number must not have been used before, but it must be unpredictable, as in the random challenge of a challenge-response protocol.

In a *Man-in-the-Middle attack*, the sender and receiver think they are talking to each other. We will abbreviate this as an MiM attack. In an MiM attack, the attacker intercepts messages from sender to receiver, in both directions. Neither sender nor receiver knows the middleman (attacker) exists.

In a confidentiality breach, the attacker may just look at the messages and not modify them. In an integrity breach, the MiM attacker can change the messages, including deleting some. In an availability attack, the MiM attacker can drop or delete messages, and not forward them to the recipient.

A *Reflection attack* is a type of Man-in-the-Middle attack. Here, the sender knows about, and speaks to, the middleman, but does not know he is an attacker. The sender sends to a receiver, who turns out to be the middleman attacker. This middleman does a concurrent protocol exchange with a third party. Using a nonce may defeat a replay attack, but may not defeat a reflection attack. Typically, the same nonce from the sender, or the third party, is used to do two concurrent transactions.

A famous example that is easy to remember is the Mafia-in-the Middle attack [6] shown in Figure 6.3. Tom wants to view a picture at the PornSite; the PornSite (which is the MiM Reflection attacker) uses Tom's credentials to buy gold coins. The protocol transactions in bold font are the communications between Tom and the PornSite. The indented, italicized protocol transactions are the transactions the PornSite has with the bank to buy gold coins with Tom's signature—but Tom is not aware of the bank (a third party) nor of this concurrent protocol transaction. Later, Tom is surprised when he sees that he has paid for gold coins.

Tom –> PornSite: Picture 43;
    PornSite –> Bank: Buy 5 gold coins;
    Bank –> PornSite: Send Signature (with challenge R);
PornSite –> Tom: Send Signature (with R) ; use the same challenge
Tom –> PornSite: Signature [R]$_{Tom}$;
    PornSite –> Bank: Signature [R]$_{Tom}$;
    Bank –> PornSite: certificate for 5 gold coins.
PornSite –> Tom: view picture 43.

Figure 6.3: Mafia-in-the-Middle Reflection attack.

In the above Reflection attack, each of the other two parties (e.g., Tom, bank) is aware that s/he is talking to the party that we call the Man-in-the-Middle (e.g., Mafia PornSite). However, none of the parties realize that this party is a MiM attacker. Also, Tom and the bank are not aware of each other.

In other (non-reflection) MiM protocol attacks, the sender and receiver are aware of each other, but not aware that there is a MiM attacker intercepting their communications. Recall that we also discussed several Man-in-the-Middle attacks in public-key protocols in Section 5.10.

There are many books [6, 7, 8, 9] and papers that deal with the security or insecurity of well-known protocols. The interested reader is advised to pursue these.

6.4 REAL-WORLD PROTOCOLS

The TLS (Transport Layer Security) protocol enables establishment of a secure channel between two parties, across the public (insecure) Internet. It was previously called the SSL (Secure Sockets Layer) protocol, and described at a conceptual level in Chapter 5. It is an example of a network protocol that first authenticates one (or both) parties in a communication over the Internet, and establishes a session key or keys, which can then be used for bulk encryption and keyed hashing, as desired, during the session.

Figure 6.4 shows the SSL handshake protocol, where the two parties negotiate and agree on various parameters for establishing a secure communications channel (secured through encryption and hashing).

1. Client –> Server: "hello", cipher list, Ra; Ra is a nonce
2. Server –> Client: cipher, Rb, server_cert, [request client_cert]; Rb is a nonce
        ; client authenticates server, gets public key PKserver from server_cert
3. Client –> Server: {S}$_{PKserver}$, E(hash(msgs, CLNT,K),K)
        ; S = pre-master secret, and K = hash(S, Ra, Rb)
4. Server –> Client: hash(msgs, SRVR, K)

Figure 6.4: SSL Handshake.

In the first two messages, the client sends the server the list of ciphers it supports, a random number Ra and any session-specific data. The server selects the cipher, generates its own random number Rb, and sends these back to the client with its own certificate, and an optional request for the client's certificate (if the client is requesting a server resource that requires client authentication). For clarity, we assume that no client authentication is required.

The client authenticates the server, and extracts the server's public key, PKserver, from the server certificate. Since the server certificate is signed by a Certificate Authority, the client's web browser should have the public key of the Certificate Authority. If the server cannot be authenticated, the user is informed that a secure channel cannot be established.

In the next two messages, the client creates the pre-master secret, S, for the session, encrypts it with the server's public key, then sends the encrypted pre-master secret to the server. The server uses its private key to decrypt the pre-master secret.

The client and server each calculates a hash over the pre-master secret, and the random numbers Ra and Rb, to generate the master secret, K. Both the client and the server use the master secret to generate the session keys, which are symmetric keys used to encrypt and decrypt information exchanged during the TLS session and to verify its integrity. (The client and server each sends a message to the other that future messages from the client will be encrypted with the session key. This is shown with the last two exchanges in Figure 6.4. Note that "msgs" means all the messages sent so far in this protocol. CLNT is a constant meaning the client is the sender of the keyed-hash value in message 3, while SRVR is a constant showing that the server is the sender of the keyed-hash value in message 4.)

If any one of the above steps fails, the TLS handshake fails and the connection is not created.

On successful completion of the above TLS handshake protocol, the session begins. The client and the server use the session keys to encrypt and decrypt the data they send to each other and to validate its integrity. This results in a secure communications channel for this session.

The HTTPS (HyperText Transfer Protocol Secure) protocol uses the SSL protocol to secure (encrypt and hash) the HTTP messages. Before sending credit-card numbers over the Internet, one should check that HTTPS is being used, rather than HTTP which sends messages in plaintext.

While the TLS protocol is at the Transport Layer of the network Protocol Stack, IPSEC (Internet Protocol SECurity) is at the Network Layer of the Protocol Stack. IPSEC consists of security protocols for enabling encryption and hashing of messages; it is integrated into the basic IP (Internet Protocol) protocol. This enables all packets to be encrypted and hashed without having to change the applications or make applications aware of the underlying encryption and hashing, as when TLS is used by the application. IPSEC is also preceded by a mutual authentication phase, which enables authentication of the sender and receiver, similar in intent to the TLS handshaking phase, but much more complicated. IPSEC is often used to establish a Virtual Private Network (VPN) across a public network. A VPN provides a cryptographically secured (hence virtually private) communications channel using encryption for confidentiality and hashing for integrity, over a public network.

6.5   VERIFYING SECURITY PROTOCOLS

In a distributed environment, e.g., Cloud Computing, it is essential to verify the security of protocols for establishing the security desired, the parameters and configurations, and for attesting to what security is actually provided. If the protocol is not secure, an attacker can use the protocol in a legitimate way to perform an attack. This is in spite of the use of very strong cryptographic algorithms and very secure key management. Hence, we must ensure that the security protocols used are not the weakest link in the security solution.

There are several tools for verifying network protocols. However, verifying hardware-software security architectures is a new area of research that is not yet well understood. Tools for security verification tend to work only for software mechanisms, or only for hardware mechanisms, but not for a hardware-software security architecture. Furthermore, these tools and also formal verification methods, do not scale to cover realistic designs. Verifying a new hardware-software security architecture requires full system simulation, which is very slow when having to simulate new hardware as well. Hopefully, we can leverage some of the network protocol verification methodology and tools, as well as tools for verifying functional correctness, to achieve security verification that cover software-hardware security architectures, and also scale to cover real systems. Furthermore, attack suites and security benchmarks are needed. Designing a methodology and a tool chain for the security verification of hardware-software security architectures is thus a very important and much needed research area. Some promising initial work in this area has been done in [43, 44, 45], but much more is needed.

CHAPTER 7

Summary

We have discussed some of the fundamental notions of security in this tutorial and introduced a systematic security architecture design methodology.

We introduced threat-based design for computer architects in Chapter 1. This complements the current performance-based, power-based, area-based and cost-based designs. In a perfect world, there would be no attackers, and security and threat-based design would not be necessary. However, in the highly interconnected, ubiquitous computing world of today and tomorrow, with ever escalating attacks, designing security-aware computers is essential. In fact, we must assume that it is unlikely our computing systems will be pristine with perfect security; rather, we should assume that they will always have some security vulnerabilities and malware in them. Yet we want to design future computers to be resilient, and to protect critical information even under attack.

We defined the cornerstone security properties of Confidentiality, Integrity and Availability (CIA), as well as many other desirable security properties. We defined a trustworthy computer to be one designed to be dependable and secure, at least with respect to the CIA triad.

We proposed a systematic way to think about the design of security-aware or trustworthy computers in the security architecture design methodology in Chapter 1. This includes identifying the user scenarios targeted, specifying the security problem succinctly, defining the threat model, designing the security mechanisms (new architectural features) and verifying the security properties at design time. At the same time, other needs like designing for performance, power optimization, cost, functionality and ease-of-use must also be considered, together with security as a first-class design goal. This may require iterating the design and evaluating tradeoffs.

In Chapter 2 we introduced security policy models for both multi-level and multi-lateral security. This summarizes the most important terminology for security policies and helps computer architects understand how to reason about security policies for protecting confidentiality or integrity. By describing only security policy models, we can understand the basic principles, rather than get lost in the many policy details found in real-life security policies couched in compliance, compatibility, legalese and domain-specific issues in a particular application domain.

Chapter 3 described basic access control, comprising authentication and authorization (AAA), and different mechanisms that have been used by Operating Systems for addressing this AAA triad. These mechanisms can also be implemented by hardware or a combination of software and hardware. For example, the SP and Bastion architectures showed how trusted software modules (TSMs) can implement arbitrary security policies in software, enforcing these policies when accessing confidential or sensitive data in cryptographically secured storage bound to these TSMs.

Chapters 4 and 5 provided an introduction to basic cryptography. There are many invaluable cryptographic techniques that the computer architect can use. In particular, instead of restricting access (as in many of the security policy models and access control mechanisms in Chapters 2 and 3), the idea is to allow free access to cryptographically protected information, except restricting the access to the cryptographic keys that allow making sense of the encrypted material.

Chapter 4 described symmetric-key ciphers and cryptographic hash algorithms. They can be used to facilitate protection of confidentiality and integrity in computer systems.

Chapter 5 described public-key cryptography, which can be used to provide longer-term digital identities for authentication and non-repudiation. The importance of digital signatures, enabled by public-key cryptography, is also discussed. Chapter 5 also discusses Public Key Infrastructure (PKI), Certificates and Certificate Authorities (CAs) which illustrate the concept of a chain of certificates, or signatures, by more trusted entities vouching for less trusted ones below them. Ultimately, the recipient should decide on the level of trust acceptable to him or her.

Chapter 6 touches upon the very subtle topic of security protocols, which are used to establish secure communications, or any secure interactions in cyberspace. These are not only network protocols, but also protocols within any distributed computing system, or even within a single physical machine. There are many aspects of security protocols, protocol attacks and protocol verification, of which we give just an initial introduction.

These chapters on security policies, access control mechanisms, cryptography algorithms and security protocols, provide the computer architect with the requisite security terminology and concepts, and a rich tool-box with which to design hardware-software security architectures.

7.1 SECURITY APPLICATIONS

Computing trends today include the Cloud Computing paradigm [45, 46, 47, 48] with smartphones and other mobile devices as the access portals, the software trend to virtualization and the hardware trend to manycore processor chips. Each of these trends presents new needs and opportunities to design security features into the basic architecture [48].

There are security needs in both general-purpose computing, e.g., servers for cloud computing data centers and smartphone clients, and special-purpose computers, e.g., embedded computers in automobile systems. The control of cyber-physical systems has not kept pace with the growth of ubiquitous networking and computing devices. Critical infrastructures like the smart power grid, transportation and water utilities all need security protections.

Social networks need privacy protections, as well as confidentiality, integrity and availability features. Online banking, purchasing, gaming, education, entertainment, etc., all require security.

The list of applications, services and technologies that need security grows; the threats also grow as attackers get more organized and sophisticated. Hence, security in our digital information world is essential and an on-going need for the future. As security defenses get better, attackers get smarter, and hence it is an on-going arms race in cyber space.

7.2   RESEARCH TOPICS IN HARDWARE SECURITY

In an attempt to keep this book short, I have restricted it to only fundamental security concepts. There are many interesting hardware-related security research topics not covered in this book, some of which I hope to cover in another book. These topics include side-channels, covert channels, information flow tracking, design for availability for both reliability and security, physically unclonable functions, secure random number generation, hardware supply-chain security, security of design tools, security verification, multicore security, FPGA security, SOC security, smartphone security, virtualization security, cloud security, embedded system security, wireless security, etc. Many of these topics require understanding or applying some of the security basics in this book, or are more advanced or specialized topics.

In general, these research topics can be placed into two major categories: designing hardware security features to enhance software and system security, or designing hardware that is itself more secure and trustworthy. An example of the former is to provide hardware support for software integrity (e.g., [25, 26, 36, 39, 40]), while an example of the latter is to design secure caches [49, 50, 51] that cannot be used as side channels to leak secret information like secret encryption keys.

7.3   THE ROAD AHEAD

Security is full of nuances, and is also subject to attack by very clever human attackers who can adapt their attacks to new defenses. Hence, it must be designed to be flexible and dynamic to meet new types of security breaches, yet it should also be non-bypassable. The advantage of hardware security mechanisms is that it can provide the non-bypassability and immutability that software defenses cannot. The advantage of software mechanisms is the flexibility and dynamic adaptability provided. Hence, a good general-purpose solution is to have hardware protect trusted software that then provides the flexible and adaptable security features, e.g., the security monitoring, security policy enforcement and other forms of flexible and adaptable security defenses. An initial step toward this goal of hardware enabling more trustworthy software was illustrated by the Bastion security architecture [36, 37].

In the future, we need security for secure cloud computing, secure smartphones, smart grid systems, automobiles, embedded systems, manycore systems, virtual machines, etc. There is a lot of past work on security—mostly in cryptography, software security and network security—that hardware and system architects can draw upon. There is also a lot of opportunity for innovation. How can we design security into systems while also improving their performance and energy efficiency?

How we computer architects meet these enormous security needs will greatly impact future computers and security in cyberspace.

Bibliography

[1]   Ruby B. Lee. Improving Cyber Security. *Advances in Cyber Security: Technology, Operations and Experiences.* Fordham University Press, pp. 37-59, 2013. Also available at palms. ee.princeton.edu/publications. 1

[2]   David E. Bell and Leonard LaPadula. Secure Computer System. ESD-TR-73-278, Mitre Corporation; v. I and II: November 1973, v. III: April 1974. 12

[3]   Kenneth J. Biba. Integrity Considerations for Secure Computer Systems. Mitre Corporation MTR-3153, 1975. 13

[4]   David F.C. Brewer and Michael J. Nash. Chinese Wall Model. Proceedings of the 1989 IEEE Symposium on Security and Privacy, pp. 215-228, 1989. DOI: 10.1109/SEC-PRI.1989.36295. 15

[5]   David Clark and David Wilson. A Comparison of Commercial and Military Computer Security Policies. Proceedings of the IEEE Symposium on Security and Privacy, pp. 184-194, 1987. DOI: 10.1109/SP.1987.10001. 17

[6]   Ross J. Anderson. *Security Engineering: a guide to building dependable distributed systems.* Second edition. John Wiley and Sons, Inc., 2008. ISBN 978-0-470-06852-6. 11, 12, 20, 32, 74

[7]   Mark Stamp. *Information Security Principles and Practice.* John Wiley and Sons, Inc. 2006. ISBN-10 0-371-73848-4. 11, 32, 56, 74

[8]   Dieter Gollmann. *Computer Security.* Wiley, 1999. ISBN 0-471-97884 2. 11, 74

[9]   Matt Bishop. *Computer Security Art and Science.* Addison Wesley. 2003. ISBN 0-201-44099-7. 11, 74

[10]   Saul Prabhakar, Sharath Pankanti and Anil Jain. Biometrics Recognition: Security and Privacy concerns. IEEE Security and Privacy, Vol. 1 No. 2, pp. 33-42, March 2003. DOI: 10.1109/MSECP.2003.1193209

[11]   Ravi Sandhu, Edward Coyne, Hal Feinstein and Charles Youman. Role-Based Access Control Models. IEEE Computer, Vol. 29 No. 2, pp. 38-47, Feb 1996. DOI: 10.1109/2.485845. 27

[12]   Richard Graubart. On the need for a third form of access control. 12th National Computer Security Conference Proceedings, pp. 293-303, October 1989. 27

[13]   C.J. McCollum, J.R. Messing and L. Notargiacomo. Beyond the pale of MAC and DAC – defining new forms of access control. IEEE Symposium on Research in Security and Privacy, pp. 190-200, 1990. DOI: 10.1109/RISP.1990.63850. 27

[14]   Yu-Yuan Chen and Ruby B. Lee. Hardware-assisted Application-level Access Control. Proceedings of the Information Security Conference (ISC), September 2009. DOI: 10.1007/978-3-642-04474-8_29. 27

[15]   Yu-Yuan Chen, Pramod Jamkhedkar and Ruby B. Lee. A Software-Hardware Architecture for Self-Protecting Data. Proceedings of the ACM conference on Computer and Communications Security (CCS), October 2012. DOI: 10.1145/2382196.2382201. 27

[16]   Shannon C. E. Communication theory of secrecy systems. Bell System Technical Journal, 28(4):656–715, 1949. 30

[17]   National Bureau of Standards. Data Encryption Standard. NBS FIPS Publication 46, January 1977. 34

[18]   National Institute of Standard and Technology. Advanced Encryption Standard (AES). FIPS 197, November 2001. 34, 36

[19]   AES Animation http://www.cs.bc.edu/~straubin/cs381-05/blockciphers/rijndael_ingles2004.swf. 36

[20]   Joan Daemen and Vincent Rijmen. *The Design of Rijndael*. Springer-Verlag ISBN:3540425802, 2002. 36

[21]   Intel. Intel advanced encryption standard instructions (AES-NI). Online: http://software.intel.com/en-us/articles/intel-advanced-encryption-standard-instructions-aes-ni/, Oct. 2010. 37

[22]   Ruby B. Lee. and Yu-Yuan Chen. Processor Accelerator for AES. Proceedings of the IEEE Symposium on Application Specific Processors, (SASP), pp. 71-76, June 2010. DOI: 10.1109/SASP.2010.5521153. 37, 46

[23]   Weidong Shi, Hsien-Hsin S. Lee, Mrinmoy Ghosh, Chenghuai Lu and Alexandra Boldyreva. High Efficiency Counter Mode Security Architecture via Prediction and Precomputation. Proceedings of the IEEE/ACM International Symposium on Computer Architecture (ISCA), 2005. DOI: 10.1145/1080695.1069972. 39

[24]   Brian Rogers, Siddhartha Chhabra, Milos Prvulovic and Yan Solihin: Using Address Independent Seed Encryption and Bonsai Merkle Trees to Make Secure Processors OS- and Performance-Friendly. Proceedings of the IEEE/ACM Symposium on Microarchitecture (MICRO), 183-196, 2007. DOI: 10.1109/MICRO.2007.16. 39, 49

[25] Ruby B. Lee, Peter C. S. Kwan, John Patrick McGregor, Jeffrey Dwoskin and Zhenghong Wang. Architecture for Protecting Critical Secrets in Microprocessors. Proceedings of the IEEE/ACM International Symposium on Computer Architecture (ISCA), pp. 2-13, June 2005. DOI: 10.1145/1080695.1069971. 40, 46, 67

[26] Jeffrey S. Dwoskin and Ruby B. Lee. Hardware-rooted Trust for Secure Key Management and Transient Trust. Proceedings of the ACM Conference on Computer and Communications Security (CCS), pp. 389-400, October 2007. DOI: 10.1145/1315245.1315294. 40, 47, 67

[27] Jeffrey S. Dwoskin, Dahai Xu, Jianwei Huang, Mung Chiang and Ruby B. Lee. Secure Key Management Architecture Against Sensor-node Fabrication Attacks. Proceedings of the IEEE GLOBECOM, Nov 2007. DOI: 10.1109/GLOCOM.2007.39. 40

[28] Dahai Xu, Jianwei Huang, Jeffrey S. Dwoskin, Mung Chiang and Ruby B. Lee. Re-examining Probabilistic Versus Deterministic Key Management. Proceedings of the IEEE International Symposium on Information Theory (ISIT), pp. 2586-2590, June 2007. DOI: 10.1109/ISIT.2007.4557608. 40

[29] Michael S. Wang and Ruby B. Lee. Architecture for a Non-Copyable Disk (NCdisk) Using a Secret-Protection (SP) SoC Solution. Proceedings of the Asilomar Conference on Signals, Systems and Computers, Nov 2007. DOI: 10.1109/ACSSC.2007.4487587. 40

[30] NIST Cryptographic Hash Algorithm Competition http://csrc.nist.gov/groups/ST/hash/sha-3/index.html. 43

[31] Ralph C. Merkle. Protocols for public key cryptography. IEEE Symposium on Security and Privacy, pages 122–134, 1980. DOI: 10.1109/SP.1980.10006. 45

[32] Blaise Gassend, G. Edward Suh, Dwaine Clarke, Marten van Dijk and Srinivas Devadas. Caches and Hash Trees for Efficient Memory Integrity. Proceedings of the IEEE International Symposium on High Performance Computer Architecture (HPCA), 2003. DOI: 10.1109/HPCA.2003.1183547. 49

[33] Reouven Elbaz, David Champagne, Catherine Gebotys, Ruby B. Lee, Nachiketh Potlapally and Lionel Torres. Hardware Mechanisms for Memory Authentication: A Survey of Existing Techniques and Engines. Transactions on Computational Science IV, Lecture Notes in Computer Science (LNCS), issue 5340, pp. 1-22, March 2009. DOI: 10.1007/978-3-642-01004-0_1. 49

[34] Alex Biryukov, Adi Shamir and David Wagner. Real Time Cryptanalysis of A5/1 on a PC. Proceedings of *Fast Software Encryption* (FSE), 2000. DOI: 10.1007/3-540-44706-7_1. 33

[35]   Elad Barkan, Eli Biham and Nathan Keller. Instant Ciphertext-only cryptanalysis of GSM encrypted communication. Technion Technical Report CS-2006-07. http://www.cs.technion.ac.il/~biham/. 33

[36]   DavidChampagne and Ruby B. Lee. Scalable Architectural Support for Trusted Software. Proceedings of the IEEE International Symposium on High-Performance Computer Architecture (HPCA), Jan 2010. DOI: 10.1109/HPCA.2010.5416657. 46, 63, 66, 67, 81

[37]   David Champagne. Scalable Security Architecture for Trusted Software.Ph.D. Thesis, Department of Electrical Engineering, Princeton University, 2010. http://palms.ee.princeton.edu/publications. 46, 63, 66, 67, 81

[38]   David Lie, Chandu Thekkath, Mark Mitchell, Patrick Lincoln, Dan Boneh, John Mitchell and Mark Horowitz. Architectural Support for Copy and Tamper Resistant Software. Proceedings of the International Conference on Architectural Support for Programming Languages and Operating Systems (ASPLOS), pages 168–177, November 2000. DOI: 10.1145/378993.379237. 48, 66

[39]   G. Edward Suh, Charles W. O'Donnell, Ishan Sachdev and Srinivas Devadas. Design and Implementation of the AEGIS Single-Chip Secure Processor Using Physical Random Functions. Proceedings of the International Symposium on Computer Architecture (ISCA), June 2005. DOI: 10.1145/1080695.1069974. 48, 66, 81

[40]   Trusted Computing Group, Trusted Platform Module (TPM) Main Specifications http://www.trustedcomputinggroup.org/resources/tpm_main_specification. 64, 81

[41]   Alfred Menezes, Paul van Oorschot, and Scott Vanstone. *The Handbook of Applied Cryptography*. CRC Press, 1996. ISBN: 0-8493-8523-7. 56, 58

[42]   Bruce Schneier. *Applied Cryptography*. 2nd Ed., John Wiley & Sons, Inc., 1996. ISBN:0-471-11709-9 56, 58

[43]   David Lie, John Mitchell, Chandramohan Thekkath and Mark Horowitz. Specifying and Verifying Hardware for Tamper-Resistant Software. Proceedings of the IEEE Symposium on Security and Privacy, May 2003. DOI: 10.1109/SECPRI.2003.1199335. 77

[44]   Mohit Tiwari, Jason Oberg, Xun Li, Jonathan K Valamehr, Timothy Levin, Ben Hardekopf, Ryan Kastner, Frederic T Chong and Timothy Sherwood. Crafting a Usable Microkernel, Processor, and I/O System with Strict and Provable Information Flow Security. Proceedings of the International Symposium of Computer Architecture (ISCA), June 2011. DOI: 10.1145/2024723.2000087. 77

[45]   Jakub Szefer. Architectures for Secure Cloud Computing Servers. Ph.D. thesis, Department of Electrical Engineering, Princeton University, May 2013. 77

[46]   Eric Keller, Jakub Szefer, Jennifer Rexford and Ruby B. Lee. NoHype: Virtu-
         alized cloud infrastructure without the virtualization. Proceedings of the IEEE/
         ACM International Symposium on Computer Architecture (ISCA), June 2010. DOI:
         10.1145/1815961.1816010. 80

[47]   Jakub Szefer, Eric Keller, Ruby B. Lee and Jennifer Rexford. Eliminating the Hypervisor
         Attack Surface for a More Secure Cloud. Proceedings of the Conference on Computer
         and Communications Security (CCS), October 2011. DOI: 10.1145/2046707.2046754.
         80

[48]   Jakub Szefer and Ruby B. Lee. Architectural Support for Hypervisor-Secure Virtu-
         alization. Proceedings of the International Conference on Architectural Support for
         Programming Languages and Operating Systems (ASPLOS), March, 2012. DOI:
         10.1145/2189750.2151022. 80

[49]   Zhenghong Wang and Ruby B. Lee. A Novel Cache Architecture with Enhanced
         Performance and Security. Proceedings of the IEEE/ACM International Sympo-
         sium on Microarchitecture (MICRO), pp. 83-93, November 2008. DOI: 10.1109/
         MICRO.2008.4771781. 81

[50]   Zhenghong Wang and Ruby B. Lee. New Cache Designs for Thwarting Software
         Cache-based Side Channel Attacks. Proceedings of the IEEE/ACM International
         Symposium on Computer Architecture (ISCA), pp. 494 - 505, June 2007. DOI:
         10.1145/1273440.1250723. 81

[51]   Leonid Domnitser, Aamer Jaleel, Jason Loew, Nael Abu-Ghazaleh and Dmitry
         Ponomarev. Non-monopolizable caches: Low-complexity mitigation of cache side chan-
         nel attacks. ACM Transactions on Architecture and Code Optimization. (TACO) 8:4,
         Article 35. January 2012. DOI: 10.1145/2086696.2086714. 81

Appendix: Further Readings

This Appendix gives some papers in Dynamic Information Flow Tracking (DIFT) (A.1), Secure Processos (A.2) and Memory Integrity Trees (A.3). The papers are listed in alphabetical order by the first author's last name.

A.1 DYNAMIC INFORMATION FLOW TRACKING (DIFT) PAPERS

[A1-1] Yu-Yuan Chen, Pramod Jamkhedkar and Ruby B. Lee. "A Software-Hardware Architecture for Self-Protecting Data." Proceedings of the ACM Conference on Computer and Communications Security (CCS), October 2012. DOI: 10.1145/2382196.2382201.

[A1-2] Jedidiah R. Crandall, Frederic T. Chong: Minos: Control Data Attack Prevention Orthogonal to Memory Model. Proceedings of the IEEE/ACM International Symposium on Microarchitecture (MICRO), 221-232, 2004. DOI: 10.1109/MICRO.2004.26.

[A1-3] Michael Dalton, Hari Kannan and Christos Kozyrakis, "Raksha: A Flexible Information Flow Architecture for Software Security", Proceedings of the International Symposium on Computer Architecture (ISCA), June 2007. DOI: 10.1145/1273440.1250722.

[A1-4] Jason Oberg, Wei Hu, Ali Irturk, Mohit Tiwari, Timothy Sherwood and Ryan Kastner. Theoretical analysis of gate level information flow tracking. Proceedings of the Design Automation Conference (DAC), pages 244-247, 2010. DOI: 10.1145/1837274.1837337.

[A1-5] Feng Qin, Cheng Wang, Zhenmin Li, Ho-seop Kim, Yuanyuan Zhou and Youfeng Wu. LIFT: A low-overhead practical information flow tracking system for detecting security attacks. Proceedings of the IEEE/ACM International Symposium on Microarchitecture (MICRO), 2006. DOI: 10.1109/MICRO.2006.29.

[A1-6] Andrei Sabelfeld and Andrew C. Myers. Language-based information-flow security. IEEE Journal on Selected Areas in Communications, Vol. 21 No. 1, January 2003. DOI: 10.1109/JSAC.2002.806121.

[A1-7] G. Edward Suh, Jaewook Lee and Srinivas Devadas. Secure Program Execution via Dynamic Information Flow Tracking. Proceedings of the International Conference on Architectural Support for Programming Languages and Operating Systems (ASPLOS), 2004. DOI: 10.1145/1024393.1024404.

[A1-8] Mohit Tiwari, Hassan M.G. Wassel, Bita Mazloom, Shashidhar Mysore, Frederic T. Chong and Timothy Sherwood. Complete information flow tracking from the gates up. Proceedings of the International Conference on Architectural Support for Programming Languages and Operating Systems (ASPLOS), pp. 109-120, 2009. DOI: 10.1145/1508244.1508258.

[A1-9] Neil Vachharajani, Matthew J. Bridges, Jonathan Chang, Ram Rangan, Guilherme Ottoni, Jason A. Blome, George A. Reis, Manish Vachharajani and David I. August. RIFLE: An architectural framework for user-centric information-flow security. Proceedings of the IEEE/ACM International Symposium on Microarchitecture, 2004. DOI: 10.1109/MICRO.2004.31.

[A1-10] Aydan R. Yumerefendi, Benjamin Mickle and Landon P. Cox. TightLip: Keeping applications from spilling the beans. Proceedings of the Symposium on Networked Systems Design and Implementation (NSDI), April 2007.

[A1-11] Nickolai Zeldovich, Hari Kannan, Michael Dalton, and Christos Kozyrakis. Hardware enforcement of application security policies using tagged memory. Proceedings of USENIX Symposium on Operating Systems Design and Implementation (OSDI), pp. 225–240, 2008.

[A1-12] Lantian Zheng and Andrew C. Myers. Dynamic security labels and static information flow control. Proceedings of the International Journal of Information Security, Vol. 6 No 2, pp. 67-84, March 2007. DOI: 10.1007/s10207-007-0019-9.

A.2 SECURE PROCESSOR PAPERS

[A2-1] Robert M. Best. Preventing Software Piracy with Crypto-microprocessors. Proceedings of the IEEE Spring COMPCON '80, pp. 466-469, 1980.

[A2-2] David Champagne. Scalable Security Architecture for Trusted Software. Ph.D. Thesis, Department of Electrical Engineering, Princeton University, 2010.

[A2-3] David Champagne and Ruby B. Lee. Scalable Architectural Support for Trusted Software. Proceedings of the IEEE International Symposium on High-Performance Computer Architecture (HPCA), January 2010. Best Paper finalist. DOI: 10.1109/HPCA.2010.5416657

[A2-4] Yu-Yuan Chen and Ruby B. Lee. Hardware-assisted Application-level Access Control. Proceedings of the Information Security Conference (ISC), September 2009. DOI: 10.1007/978-3-642-04474-8_29.

[A2-5]   Jeffrey S Dwoskin and Ruby B. Lee. Hardware-rooted Trust for Secure Key Management and Transient Trust. Proceedings of the ACM Conference on Computer and Communications Security (CCS), pp. 389-400, October 2007. DOI: 10.1145/1315245.1315294.

[A2-6]   Jeffrey Dwoskin, Dahai Xu, Jianwei Huang, Mung Chiang and Ruby B. Lee. Secure Key Management Architecture Against Sensor-node Fabrication Attacks. Proceedings of IEEE GLOBECOMM, Nov 2007. DOI: 10.1109/GLOCOM.2007.39

[A2-7]   Tanguy Gilmont, John-Didier Legat and Jean-Jacques Quisquater. An Architecture of Security Management Unit for Safe Hosting of Multiple Agents. Proceedings of the International Workshop on Intelligent Communications and Multimedia Terminals, pp. 79-82, November 1998.

[A2-8]   Peter Gutmann. An Open-source Cryptographic Coprocessor. Proceedings of the USENIX Security Symposium, 2000.

[A2-9]   Darko Kirovski, Milenko Drinic and Miodrag Potkonjak. Enabling Trusted Software Integrity. Proceedings of the International Conference on Architectural Support for Programming Languages and Operating Systems (ASPLOS), October 2002. DOI: 10.1145/605397.605409.

[A2-10] Hugo Krawczyk. The Order of Encryption and Authentication for Protecting Communications (or: How Secure Is SSL?). Proceedings of CRYPTO 2001. LNCS 2139, pp. 310-331, 2001. DOI: 10.1007/3-540-44647-8_19.

[A2-11] Ruby B. Lee, David K. Karig, John P. McGregor and Zhijie Shi. Enlisting hardware architecture to thwart malicious code injection. Proceedings of the International Conference on Security in Pervasive Computing, 2003. DOI: 10.1007/978-3-540-39881-3_21.

[A2-12] Ruby B. Lee, Peter C. S. Kwan, John Patrick McGregor, Jeffrey Dwoskin and Zhenghong Wang. Architecture for Protecting Critical Secrets in Microprocessors. Proceedings of the IEEE/ACM International Symposium on Computer Architecture (ISCA), pp. 2-13, June 2005. DOI: 10.1109/ISCA.2005.14.

[A2-13] David Lie, John Mitchell, Chandramohan Thekkath and Mark Horowitz. Specifying and Verifying Hardware for Tamper-Resistant Software. Proceedings of the IEEE Symposium on Security and Privacy. May 2003. DOI: 10.1109/SECPRI.2003.1199335.

[A2-14] David Lie, Chandramohan Thekkath and Mark Horowitz. Implementing an untrusted operating system on trusted hardware. Proceedings of the ACM Symposium on Operating Systems Principles (SOSP), pp. 178–192, Oct. 2003. Best Paper award. DOI: 10.1145/1165389.945463.

[A2-15] David Lie, Chandu Thekkath, Patrick Lincoln, Mark Mitchell, Dan Boneh, John Mitchell, Mark Horowitz. Architectural Support for Copy and Tamper Resistant Software. Proceedings of the International Conference on Architectural Support for Programming Languages and Operating Systems (ASPLOS), pp. 168–177, November 2000. DOI: 10.1145/378993.379237.

[A2-16] John P. McGregor and Ruby B. Lee. Protecting Cryptographic Keys and Computations via Virtual Secure Coprocessing. Workshop on Architectural Support for Security and Antivirus (WASSA), Oct 2004; also in Computer Architecture News, ACM Press, Vol. 33. No. 1, pp 16-26, Mar 2005. DOI: 10.1145/1055626.1055630.

[A2-17] Brian Rogers, Siddhartha Chhabra, Yan Solihin and Milos Prvulovic. Using Address Independent Seed Encryption and Bonsai Merkle Trees to Make Secure Processors OS- and Performance-Friendly. Proceedings of the IEEE/ACM International Symposium on Microarchitecture (MICRO), 2007. DOI: 10.1109/MICRO.2007.44.

[A2-18] Sean W. Smith, Elaine R. Palmer and Steve H. Weingart. Using a High-Performance, Programmable Secure Coprocessor. Proceedings of the International Conference on Financial Cryptography, pp.73-89, 1998. DOI: 10.1007/BFb0055474.

[A2-19] Sean W. Smith and Steve H. Weingart. Building a High-Performance, Programmable Secure Coprocessor. Computer Networks, 31(8), pp. 831-860, April 1999.

[A2-20] SP and Bastion Secure Processor Architectures web-page: http://palms.ee.princeton.edu/sp_bastion

[A2-21] G Edward Suh, Dwaine Clarke, Blaise Gassend, Marten Van Dijk and Srinivas Devadas. AEGIS: Architecture for Tamper-Evident and Tamper-Resistant Processing. Proceedings of the International Conference on Supercomputing (MIT-CSAIL-CSG-Memo-474 is an updated version), June 2003. DOI: 10.1145/782814.782838.

[A2-22] G. Edward Suh, Charles W. O'Donnell, Ishan Sachdev, and Srinivas Devadas. Design and Implementation of the AEGIS Single-Chip Secure Processor Using Physical Random Functions. Proceedings of the IEEE/ACM International Symposium on Computer Architecture (ISCA), June 2005. DOI: 10.1145/1080695.1069974.

[A2-23] J. Doug Tygar and Bennet Yee. Dyad: A System for Using Physically Secure Coprocessors. Carnegie Mellon University Technical Report CMU-CS-91-140R, May 1991.

[A2-24] Xiaolan Zhang, Leendert Doorn, Trent Jaeger, R. Perez and Reiner Sailer. Secure coprocessor-based intrusion detection. Proceedings of the ACM SIGOPS European workshop, pp. 239-242, September 2002. DOI: 10.1145/1133373.1133423.

A.3 MEMORY INTEGRITY TREE PAPERS

[A3-1] David Champagne, Reouven Elbaz and Ruby B. Lee. The Reduced Address Space for Application Memory Authentication. Proceedings of the Information Security Conference (ISC), September 2008. DOI: 10.1007/978-3-540-85886-7_4.

[A3-2] Dwaine E. Clarke, Srinivas Devadas, Marten van Dijk, Blaise Gassend and G. Edward Suh. Incremental Multiset Hash Functions and Their Application to Memory Integrity Checking. Proceedings of ASIACRYPT, pp. 188-207, 2003. DOI: 10.1007/978-3-540-40061-5_12.

[A3-3] Dwaine E. Clarke, G. Edward Suh, Blaise Gassend, Ajay Sudan, Marten van Dijk and Srinivas Devadas. Toward Constant Bandwidth Overhead Integrity Checking of Untrusted Data. Proceedings of the IEEE Symposium on Security and Privacy, pp. 139-153, 2005. DOI: 10.1.1.113.3014.

[A3-4] Reouven Elbaz, David Champagne, Catherine Gebotys, Ruby B. Lee, Nachiketh Potlapally and Lionel Torres. Hardware Mechanisms for Memory Authentication: A Survey of Existing Techniques and Engines. Transactions on Computational Science IV, Lecture Notes in Computer Science (LNCS), issue 5340, pp. 1-22, March 2009. Special Issue on Security in Computing. DOI: 10.1.1.156.1082.

[A3-5] Reouven Elbaz, David Champagne, Ruby B. Lee, Lionel Torres, Gilles Sassatelli and Peter Guillemin. TEC-Tree: A Low Cost, Parallelizable Tree for Efficient Defense against Memory Replay Attacks. Proceedings of Cryptographic Hardware and Embedded Systems (CHES), pp. 289-302, September 2007. DOI: 10.1007/978-3-540-74735-2_20.

[A3-6] Blaise Gassend, G. Edward Suh, Dwaine Clarke, Marten van Dijk and Srinivas Devadas. Caches and Hash Trees for Efficient Memory Integrity. Proceedings of the IEEE International Symposium on High Performance Computer Architecture (HPCA), 2003. DOI: 10.1109/HPCA.2003.1183547.

[A3-7] Eric Hall and Charanjit S. Jutla. Parallelizable Authentication Trees. Cryptology ePrint Archive. DOI: 10.1.1.12.227.

[A3-8] Ralph C. Merkle. Protocols for public key cryptography. Proceedings of the IEEE Symposium on Security and Privacy, pp. 122–134, 1980.

[A3-9] Brian Rogers, Siddhartha Chhabra, Yan Solihin and Milos Prvulovic. Using Address Independent Seed Encryption and Bonsai Merkle Trees to Make Secure Processors OS- and Performance-Friendly. Proceedings of the IEEE/ACM International Symposium on Microarchitecture (MICRO), 2007. DOI: 10.1109/MICRO.2007.44.

[A3-10] Brian Rogers, Yan Solihin and Milos Prvulovic. Efficient Data Protection for Distributed Shared Memory Multiprocessors. Proceedings of the International Conference on Parallel Architectures and Compilation Techniques (PACT), 2006. DOI: 10.1145/1152154.1152170.

[A3-11] Brian Rogers, Chenyu Yan, Siddhartha Chhabra, Milos Prvulovic and Yan Solihin. Single-Level Integrity and Confidentiality Protection for Distributed Shared Memory Multiprocessors. Proceedings of the IEEE International Symposium on High Performance Computer Architecture (HPCA), Feb 2008. DOI: 10.1109/HPCA.2008.4658636.

[A3-12] Weidong Shi, Hsien-Hsin S Lee, Mrinmoy Ghosh, Chenghuai Lu and Alexandra Boldyreva. High Efficiency Counter Mode Security Architecture via Prediction and Precomputation. Proceedings of the IEEE/ACM International Symposium on Computer Architecture (ISCA), 2005. DOI: 10.1145/1080695.1069972.

[A3-13] G. Edward Suh, Dwaine Clarke, Blaise Gasend, Marten Van Dijk and Srinivas Devadas. Efficient Memory Integrity Verification and Encryption for Secure Processors. Proceedings of the IEEE/ACMAnnual International Symposium on Microarchitecture (MICRO), 2003. DOI: 10.1109/MICRO.2003.1253207.

[A3-14] Chenyu Yan, Daniel Englender, Milos Prvulovic, Brian Rogers and Yan Solihin. Improving Cost, Performance, and Security of Memory Encryption and Authentication. Proceedings of the IEEE/ACM International Symposium on Computer Architecture (ISCA), 2006. DOI: 10.1109/ISCA.2006.22.

Author's Biography

Ruby B. Lee is the Forrest G. Hamrick professor of engineering and professor of electrical engineering at Princeton University, with an affiliated appointment in computer science. She is the director of the Princeton Architecture Laboratory for Multimedia and Security (PALMS). Her current research is in designing computer architecture for security and resilience, protecting critical data, securing cloud computing and smartphones, designing trustworthy hardware, secure caches and and secure multicore chips, and security verification. Hardware-enhanced security architectures designed at her PALMS research group include the SP and Bastion secure processor architectures, the Newcache and other secure cache architectures, the NoHype and Hyperwall secure cloud servers, the DataSafe architecture for self-protecting data, and novel instructions for accelerating ciphers and bit permutations.

Lee is a fellow of the ACM and the IEEE, and has served as associate editor-in-chief of *IEEE Micro*, editorial board member of *IEEE Security and Privacy* and advisory board member of *IEEE Spectrum.*. She has served as the hardware security expert on national committees on cybersecurity research, such as the National Academies committee to help improve cyber security research in the U. S., and as a co-chair for the National Cyber Leap Year summit, which resulted in calls for security research proposal funding from several agencies. She has been granted more than 120 U. S. and international patents, and has authored numerous conference papers with several awards.

Prior to joining Princeton, Lee served as chief architect at Hewlett-Packard, responsible at different times for processor architecture, multimedia architecture, and security architecture. She was a founding architect of HP's PA-RISC architecture and instrumental in the initial design of several generations of PA-RISC processors for HP's business and technical computer product lines. She also helped the widespread adoption of multimedia in commodity products by pioneering multimedia support in microprocessors and producing the first real-time software MPEG video in low-end commodity products. She was co-leader of the 64-bit Intel-HP multimedia architecture team. She created the first security roadmap for enterprise and e-commerce security for HP before going to Princeton. Simultaneous with her full-time HP tenure, she was also consulting professor of electrical engineering at Stanford University. She has a Ph.D. in electrical engineering and an M.S. in computer science, both from Stanford University, and an A.B. with distinction from Cornell University, where she was a College Scholar.